SOCIAL WORK WITH THE
FIRST NATIONS

a comprehensive bibliography
with annotations

compiled by

JOYCE Z. WHITE

COUNCIL ON SOCIAL WORK EDUCATION
ALEXANDRIA, VIRGINIA

for **Pi'sum wayapi** *and* **Waawaashkeshi**

Council on Social Work Education
1725 Duke Street, Suite 500
Alexandria, VA 22314-3457

Printed in the United States of America

Social Work with the First Nations: A Comprehensive Bibliography with Annotations

Compiled by Joyce Z. White

ISBN 0-87293-085-8

CONTENTS

INTRODUCTION

This bibliography grew out of numerous requests for curriculum and training materials for social work and human services practice with First Nations. The term First Nations is chosen as a more empowering descriptor for the indigenous peoples of this continent and their descendants than phrases such as Indian, American Indian, or Native American. Yellow Bird (1999) notes that the latter are not accurate and serve to maintain oppression. Since there is no universally accepted term used among native peoples, I have tried to be consistent in using the descriptor preferred by the author or authors of the works cited.

The bibliography is designed to be user-friendly. It is assumed that most readers will prefer to turn to a topic area for specific information, rather than look through the entire work. Because of this, there is some repetition of citations under different topic areas. When this work was originally conceived, there was some discussion of arranging references by the five social work curriculum sequences: HBSE, Policy, Research, Practice, and Field. This was not feasible as many of the articles, books, and films could be used in more than one sequence.

The topics I have chosen to use reflect materials available in the literature, the media, and on the Internet. Some areas, such as substance abuse, have been extensively researched and offer a plethora of publications and materials from which to choose, whereas others have attracted little scholarly attention. The topics covered here are: Adolescents and Children, Administration, Management, and Supervision; Aging; Alcoholism and Substance Abuse; Child Welfare: Indian Child Welfare Act; Culture, Values, and Identity; Disability Including Special Education; Deaf and Hard of Hearing; Domestic Violence; Professional and University Education; Primary and Secondary Education; Empowerment; Families; Fetal Alcohol Syndrome; Health; Maternal-Child Health; HIV/AIDS; Homelessness; Mental Health; Parenting; Policy, History, and Social Welfare; Practice; Research; Sexual Orientation; Spirituality and Religion; Suicide; Urban Issues; Veterans; Vocational Rehabilitation and Work; and Women. There is an additional section of citations from the World Wide Web which are, unfortunately, constantly changing. Selections were based on the author's assessment of their general usefulness to the average practitioner, teacher, or student. Brief annotations were added when the focus of the text was not immediately clear from the title. It should be noted that this is not meant to be a comprehensive reference work, and the reader is referred to the many bibliographies already available for in-depth research on areas of interest such as tribal histories, treaties, and the like.

I wish to thank Mike Jacobsen and Hilary Weaver for sharing their earlier unpublished bibliography, and Michael Yellow Bird for providing annotations for his publications.

ADOLESCENTS AND CHILDREN

Abraham, K. (1984). Navajo and Anglo child rearing behaviors: Cross-cultural comparison. *Journal of Comparative Family Studies, 15*(3), 373-388.

American Indian Law Center. (1981). *Model children's code (2nd ed.) and children's court rules.* Albuquerque, NM: Author.

Anderson, S. C. (1983). *Indian child welfare: Resources and references.* Norman, OK: University of Oklahoma School of Social Work.

Ashbranner, B., & Conklin, P. (1984). *To live in two worlds: American Indian youth today.* New York: Dodd-Mead.

> This is a series of interviews with young native high school and college students. Students discuss the future, their careers, their identity, and their cultural backgrounds. Photographs are included.

Ashby, M. R., Gilchrist, L. D., & Miramontez, A. (1987). Group treatment for sexually abused American Indian adolescents. *Social Work With Groups, 10*(4), 21-31.

> This article describes a program for group counseling of sexually abused American Indian girls. The program made use of traditional cultural values and reported positive outcomes.

Barlow, A., & Walkup, J. T. (1998). Developing mental health services for Native American children. *Child and Adolescent Psychiatric Clinics of North America, 7*(3), 555-577.

> Native American children need culturally relevant services. This article suggests ways to provide mental health services within the context of contemporary American Indian life.

Bates, S. C., Beauvais, F., & Trimble, J. E. (1997). American Indian adolescent alcohol involvement and ethnic identification. *Substance Use and Misuse, 32*(14), 2013-2031.

> In a sample of over 200 adolescents, results showed that ethnic identity does not predict alcohol involvement. Peer alcohol associations and family sanctions against alcohol use do appear to be predictive. Explanations of American Indian adolescents' use of alcohol are explored in light of these findings.

Beals, J., Piasecki, J., Nelson, S., Jones, M., Keane, E., Daphinais, P., Shirt, R. R., Sack, W. H., & Manson, S. M. (1997). Psychiatric disorder among American Indian adolescents: Relevance in Northern Plains youth. *Journal of the American Academy of Child and Adolescent Psychiatry, 36*(9), 1252-1259.

> This survey of psychiatric disorders among 14 to 16 year-old adolescents attending reservation schools indicates high rates of substance abuse and psychiatric and related disorders.

Beauvais, F. (1992a). An integrated model for prevention and treatment of drug abuse among American Indian youth. *Journal of Addictive Diseases, 11*(3), 68-80.

Beauvais, F. (1992b). Trends in Indian adolescent drug and alcohol abuse. *American Indian and Alaska Native Mental Health Research, 5*(1), 1-12.

Beauvais, F., Oetting, E. R., & Edwards, R. W. (1985a). Trends in drug use of Indian adolescents living on reservations, 1975-1983. *American Journal on Drug and Alcohol Dependence, 11*(3), 209-229.

Beauvais, F., Oetting, E. R., & Edwards, R. W. (1985b). Trends in the use of inhalants among American Indian adolescents. *White Cloud Journal of American Indian Mental Health, 3*(4), 3-11.

Beiser, M., Sack, W., Manson, S. M., Redshirt, R., & Dion, R. (1998). Mental health and the academic performance of First Nations and majority culture children. *Journal of Orthopsychiatry, 68*(3), 455-467.

> **The authors show that children's verbal IQs and their beliefs about personal competence contribute to whether they will be successful in majority culture schools.**

Berlin, I. N. (1984). Prevention of emotional problems among Native American children: An overview of developmental issues. *Progress in Child Psychiatry and Child Development, 41*(2), 320-333.

Blanchard, E., & Barch, R. L. (1980). What is best for tribal children: A response to Fishler. *Social Work, 25*(5), 350-357.

> **The author defends the Indian Child Welfare Act in a response to an article in the same issue by R. S. Fishler entitled "Protecting American Indian children." Fishler argued that the Indian Child Welfare Act did not adequately protect native children.**

Brendtro, L. K. (1991). The circle of courage. *Beyond Behavior, 2*(1), 5-12.

> **The author gives an introduction to American Indian views on child development.**

Broadhurst, D. D., & Tuthill, N. M. (1984). *Improving permanency outcome for American Indian and Alaskan Native children: Training curriculum and participant manual.* Albuquerque, NM: American Indian Law Center.

Center for Social Research and Development. (1976). *Indian child welfare: A state-of-the-field study and summary of findings and discussion of policy implications.* Denver, CO: Graduate School of Social Work, University of Denver.

Challenges confronting American Indian youth: Oversight hearing before the Committee on Indian Affairs, 101st Congress, First Session (1995).

> **Native American youths' testimony before the Senate Committee on Indian Affairs. This is an overview in their own words of problems facing American Indian young people.**

Circle of life [VHS]. (1990). (Available from Leech Lake Reservation, Health Division, Cass Lake, MN)

> **Teens discuss and give advice about substance abuse, teen pregnancy and parenting, and violence in relationships.**

Circle of life: Wellness and sexuality [VHS]. (1989). (Available from Planned Parenthood of Central Oklahoma, Oklahoma City, OK)

American Indian teens discuss relationships, AIDS, and pregnancy in the life of a young couple who meet at a native gathering.

Collinge, W. B. (1984). *A bibliography on Native American child and family welfare*. Berkeley, CA: University of Berkeley School of Social Welfare.

Bibliography through 1982 on American Indian children and families, with a topical index. It contains over 600 entries and 200 topics.

Commission on State-Tribal Relations. (1981). *Indian Child Welfare Act case studies and state implementation of the Indian Child Welfare Act*. Albuquerque, NM: Author.

Costello, E. J., Farmer, E. M., Angold, A., Burns, B. J., & Erkankli, A. (1997). Psychiatric disorders among American Indian and white youth in Appalachia: The Great Smoky Mountains study. *American Journal of Public Health, 87*(5), 827-832.

The authors find that psychiatric disorders among 9, 11, and 13 year-old children in the study were similar in prevalence across racial and ethnic groups, although substance abuse and psychiatric disorder were more frequent among the American Indian young people. Additionally, American Indian children were found to use fewer mental health services than other children. American Indian families also experience higher rates of poverty, unemployment, and violence than whites, but family mental illness other than substance abuse is lower. The authors explain that poverty does not appear to play the same role in American Indian families as it does among whites, and poverty and crime may, therefore, play a different etiologic role in child psychiatric disorders in the different communities.

Cross, T. (1986). Drawing on cultural tradition in Indian child welfare practice. *Social Casework, 67*(5), 283-289.

Cummins, J. R., Ireland, M., Resnick, M. D., & Blum, R. W. (1999). Correlates of physical and emotional health among Native American adolescents. *Journal of Adolescent Health, 24*(1), 38-44.

Risk factors and protective factors are analyzed by gender for physical and emotional health among American Indian youth.

Davis, S. M., Hunt, K., & Kitzes, J. M. (1989). Improving the health of Indian teenagers: A demonstration program in rural New Mexico. *Public Health Reports, 104*(3), 271-278.

DeBruyn, L. M., Lujan, C. C., & May, P. A. (1992). A comparative study of abused and neglected American Indian children in the southwest. *Social Science and Medicine, 35*(3), 305-315.

This study finds that alcohol abuse is correlated with child abuse and neglect in the family, but is not the sole cause.

Dinges, N.G., & Duong-Tran, O. (1992/93). Stressful life events and co-occurring depression, substance abuse, and suicidality among American Indian and Alaska Native adolescents. *Culture, Medicine and Psychiatry, 16*(4), 487-502.

Duclos, C. W., Beals, J., Novins, D. K., Martin, C., Jewett, C. S., & Manson, S. M. (1998). Prevalence of common psychiatric disorders among American Indian adolescent detainees. *Journal of the American Academy of Child and Adolescent Psychiatry, 37*(8), 866-873.

In a sample of 150 youngsters detained in a reservation-based center over a one year period, a high number were found to have psychiatric disorders.

Duryea, E. J., & Matzek, S. (1990). Results of a first-year pilot study in peer pressure management among American Indian youth. *Wellness Perspectives: Research, Theory, and Practice, 27*(2), 17-30.

Fishler, R. S. (1980). Protecting American Indian children. *Social Work, 25,* 341-349.

The author states that the Indian Child Welfare Act does not protect Indian children. There is a response by Blanchard and Barsh entitled "What is best for children: A response to Fischler" in the same issue.

Foerster, L. M. (1974). Open education and Native American values. *Educational Leadership, 32*(1), 41-45.

Open classrooms are found to be compatible with traditional Native American values and ways of life.

Foerster, L. M. (1977). Trends in early childhood education for Native American pupils. *Educational Leadership, 34*(5), 373-378.

Foster, P. A., Bacon, K. G., & Storck, M. (1998). Teacher, parent and youth report of problem behaviors among rural American Indian and Caucasian adolescents. *American Indian and Alaska Native Mental Health Research, 8*(2), 1-23.

The author discovers that problem behaviors of American Indian and Caucasian youth appear to be similar.

Garret, J. T. (1993/94). Understanding Indian children, learning from Indian elders. *Children Today, 22*(4), 18.

Gilchrist, L., Schinke, S. P., Trimble, J. E., & Cvetkovich, G. (1987). Skills enhancement to prevent substance abuse among American Indian adolescents. *International Journal of the Addictions, 22*(9), 869-879.

Goldstein, J., & Goldstein, S. (1996). "Put yourself in the skin of the child," she said. *Psychoanalytic Study of the Child, 51,* 46-55.

This is a case of two American Indian children adopted by a non-Indian family that came before the U.S. Supreme Court and an Indian Tribal Court. The authors discuss issues of transcultural adoption and contested placements.

Goodluck, C. (1993). Social services with Native Americans: Current status of the Indian Child Welfare Act. In H. P. MacAdoo (Ed.), *Family ethnicity: Strength in diversity* (pp. 217 – 226). Thousand Oaks, CA: Sage.

Goodluck, C. (1995). Is transracial adoption harmful to a child's development? In R. L. DelCampo & D. S. DelCampo (Eds.), *Taking sides: Clashing views on controversial issues in childhood and society* (pp. 55-67). Guilford, CT: Dushkin Publishers.

Goodluck, C. (1995/1996). *Seventh generation youth project: Fifteen session curriculum.* Denver, CO: University of Denver Graduate School of Social Work.

Goodluck, C. (1996). *Seventh generation youth project: Six session booster curriculum.* Denver, CO: University of Denver Graduate School of Social Work.

Goodluck, C. (1998). *Understanding Navajo ethnic identity: Weaving the meaning through the voices of young girls.* Unpublished doctoral dissertation: University of Denver, Graduate School of Social Work.

Goodluck, C., & Bane, W. (1984). *American Indian youth resource guide.* Denver, CO: University of Denver, Family Resource Center.

Goodluck, C., & Brown, M. E. (n.d.). *Decision making regarding American Indian children in foster care.* Denver, CO: University of Denver, Graduate School of Social Work.

Goodluck, C. T., & Edkstein, F. (1978). American Indian adoption programs: An ethnic approach to child welfare. *White Cloud Journal of American Indian Mental Health, 1*(1), 3-6.

Goodluck, C., & Martin, S. (1991). *Adoption source book.* Denver, CO: University of Denver, Family Resource Center, Region VIII.

Goodluck, C., & McGuire, R. (1997). *Seventh generation project: Booster session for sixth and seventh graders curriculum.* Denver, CO: University of Denver, Graduate School of Social Work.

Goodluck, C. T., & Short, D. (1980). Working with American Indian parents: A cultural approach. *Social Casework, 61*(5), 472-475.

Grandboise, G. H. (1980). *Indian child welfare: A beginning.* Omaha, NE: University of Nebraska, Omaha, School of Social Work.

Gray, E., & Cosgrove, J. (1985). Ethnocentric perception of child rearing practices in protective services. *Child Abuse and Neglect, 9*(2), 386-396.

> **Protective services workers are not always aware of cultural differences in raising children, and the authors find that this leads to institutional abuse of minority families. Child-rearing practices of six groups, including Blackfeet, are discussed.**

Gray, N. (1998). Addressing trauma in substance abuse treatment with American Indian adolescents. *Journal of Substance Abuse Treatment, 15*(5), 393-399.

> **The author discovers that substance abuse and trauma are correlates, suggesting the need for treatment to focus on issues of loss and trauma.**

Grossman, D. C., Putsch, R. W., & Inui, T. S. (1993). The meaning of death to adolescents in an American Indian community. *Family Medicine, 25*(9), 593-597.

> **There is a high mortality rate among young people in American Indian populations. The authors explore beliefs about death, sickness, and healing (including Spirit Sickness).**

Henderson, E., Kunitz, S. J., Gabriel, K. R., McCright, A., & Levy, J. (1998). Boarding and public schools: Navajo educational attainment, conduct disorder, and alcohol dependency. *American Indian and Alaska Native Mental Health Research, 8*(2), 24-45.

> **While there is a widespread belief that there is a relationship between boarding school attendance and alcohol dependency, this study of over 1,000 Navajo finds no such correlation.**

Herring, R. D. (1989). Counseling Native-American children: Implications for elementary school counselors. *Elementary School Guidance and Counseling, 23*(4), 272-281.

Horesji, C., & Craig, B. (1992). Reactions by Native American parents to child protection agencies: Cultural and community factors. *Child Welfare, 71*(4), 329.

> **The authors investigate how cultural experiences of oppression affect the ability of native parents to provide appropriate parenting or to accept help from government agencies and staff.**

Hyn, G. W., & Garcia, W. I. (1992). Intellectual assessment of the Native American student. *School Psychology Digest, 8*(4), 446-454.

> **Cultural experiences of American Indian children affect research and clinical findings and should be taken into account when research is interpreted. The authors give recommendations.**

Hynd, G. W. (1979). Clinical utility of the WISCR and the French Pictorial Test of Intelligence with Native American primary grade children. *Perceptual and Motor Skills, 49*(2), 480-482.

> **The author evaluates cultural bias in the use of these scales.**

Ishisaka, H. (1978). American Indians and foster care: Cultural factors and separation. *Child Welfare, 57*(5), 299-306.

> **Cultural factors may play a major role in the decision to remove children from Indian families. Twenty-six native families were provided with intensive services including apartments in a residential facility, employment, advocacy and treatment for various disorders.The goal was to prevent damage to children created by placement in foster care.**

Johnson, B. B. (1981). The Indian Child Welfare Act of 1978: Implications for practice. *Child Welfare, 60*(7), 435-446.

Jones, M. C., Dauphinais, M., Sack, W. H., & Somervell, P. D. (1997). Trauma-related symptomatology among American Indian adolescents. *Journal of Traumatic Stress, 10*(2), 163-173.

> **This study looks at symptoms related to trauma in a sample of 109 young people.**

Keltner, B. R. (1993). Native American children and adolescents: Cultural distinctiveness and cultural needs. *Journal of Child and Adolescent Psychiatric and Mental Health Nursing, 6*(4), 18-23.

> **Oppression and poverty are correlated with mental and emotional difficulties in this population. The authors insist that sensitivity to cultural difference and need is required.**

Kessel, J. A., & Robbins, S. P. (1984). The Indian Child Welfare Act: Dilemmas and needs. *Child Welfare, 63*(3), 225-232.

King, J., & Thayer, J. F. (1997). Examining conceptual models for understanding drug use behavior among American Indian youth. *Substance Use and Misuse, 32*(12/13), 1937-1942.

The authors propose models for intervention with adolescent substance abuse in a boarding school population.

Lazarus, P. J. (1982). Counseling the Native American child: A question of values. *Elementary School Guidance and Counseling, 17*(2), 83-88.

Liu, L. L., Slap, G. B., Kinsman, S. B., & Kahlid, N. (1994). Pregnancy among American Indian adolescents: Reactions and prenatal care. *Journal of Adolescent Health, 15*(4), 336-341.

American Indian teens are twice as likely as other teens to have children and these pregnancies are also more likely to be unplanned. The authors explore barriers to receiving care.

Lodico, M. A., Gruber, E., & DiClemente, R. J. (1996). Childhood sexual abuse and coercive sex among school-based adolescents in a midwestern state. *Journal of Adolescent Health, 18*(3), 211-217.

Long, K. (1986). Suicide intervention and prevention with Indian adolescents. *Issues in Mental Health Nursing, 8*(3), 247-253.

Lujan, C. C., DeBruyn, B., May, P. A., & Bird, M. E. (1989). Profile of abused and neglected Indian children in the southwest. *Child Abuse and Neglect, 13*(4), 449-461.

Ma, G. X., Toubbeh, J., & Cline, J. (1998). Native American adolescents' view of fetal alcohol prevention in schools. *Journal of School Health, 68*(4), 131-136.

Pre-teen and early teen American Indian students were asked about prevention of fetal alcohol syndrome. One-half of the group had used alcohol and the majority felt prevention was important. The authors propose creative strategies for outreach to this age group.

Mannes, M. (1993). Seeking the balance between child protection and family preservation in Indian child welfare. *Child Welfare, 72*(2), 141-152.

McLeod, J. D., & Edwards, K. (1995). Contextual determinants of children's' responses to poverty. *Social Forces, 73*(4), 1487-1508.

The authors state that the impact of poverty and neighborhood environment on Native American children is more significant than for whites or African Americans.

Mitchell, C. M., & Beals, J. (1997). The structure of problem and positive behavior among American Indian adolescents: Gender and community differences. *American Journal of Community Psychology, 25*(3), 257-288.

A sample of almost two thousand native adolescents was conducted, producing information the authors believe to be of value in prevention and research efforts.

Mitchell, C. M., Novins, D. K., & Holmes, T. (1999). Marijuana use among American Indian adolescents: A growth-curve analysis from ages 14 through 20 years. *Journal of the American Academy of Child and Adolescent Psychiatry, 38*(1), 72-78.

> **This sample of 1,770 young people over a three-year period shows a clear developmental pathway in the use of this drug. Use peaked in late adolescence and began to decrease in early adulthood.**

Moran, J., Fleming, C., Somervell, P., & Manson, S. (in press). Measuring ethnic identity among American Indian adolescents. *Journal of Research on Adolescence.*

Morey, S. M., & Gilliam, O. L. (Eds.). (1974). *Respect for life: The traditional upbringing of American Indian children.* Garden City, NY: Waldorf Press.

Myers, J. A. (Ed.). (1981). *They are young once but Indian forever: A summary and analysis of investigative hearings on Indian child welfare, April, 1980.* Oakland, CA: American Indian Lawyer Training Program.

Novins, D. K., Beals, J., & Manson, S. M. (1996). Substance abuse treatment of American Indian adolescents: Comorbid symptomatology, gender differences, and treatment patterns. *Journal of the American Academy of Child and Adolescent Psychiatry, 35*(12), 1593-1601.

> **Over two-thirds of youngsters in this study had one or more psychiatric symptoms. Females were more likely to be victims of abuse and to report substance abuse. They were also more likely to receive treatment.**

Novins, D. K., Bechtold, D. W., Sack, W., Thompson, J., Carter, D. R., & Manson, S. M. (1997). The DSM-IV outline for cultural formulation: A critical demonstration with American Indian children. *Journal of the American Academy of Child and Adolescent Psychiatry, 36*(9), 1244-1251.

> **This article provides information specific to the use of the *Diagnostic and Statistical Manual of Mental Disorders* with American Indian children and adolescents as a population.**

Novins, D. K., Harman, C. P., Mitchell, C. M., & Manson, S. M. (1996). Factors associated with the receipt of alcohol treatment services among American Indian adolescents. *Journal of the American Academy of Child and Adolescent Psychiatry, 35*(1), 110-117.

> **Over 2,000 American Indian adolescents were surveyed in a five-year period. The authors found that there is a strong association between recommendation for treatment and receipt of treatment.**

Novins, D. K., & Mitchell, C. M. (1998). Factors associated with marijuana use among American Indian adolescents. *Addiction, 93*(11), 1693-1702.

> **This is a study of 1,400 native teens in four tribes, and correlates of their use of marijuana. The use of alcohol and other drugs was among factors most closely correlated with use of cannabis.**

Nybell, L. M. (1984). *Serving American Indian families and children: A sourcebook in child welfare.* Ann Arbor, MI: National Child Welfare Training Center, University of Michigan, School of Social Work.

Oetting, E. R., & Beauvais, F. (1990/1991). Orthogonal cultural identification theory: The cultural identification of minority adolescents. *International Journal of the Addictions, 25*(5a/6a), 655-685.

Oetting, E. R., Beauvais, F., & Edwards, R. W. (1988). Alcohol and Indian youth: Social and psychological correlates and prevention. *Journal of Drug Issues, 18*(1), 87-101.

Oetting, E. R., Swaim, R. C., Edwards, R. W., & Beauvais, F. (1989). Indian and Anglo adolescent alcohol use and emotional distress: Path models. *American Journal of Drug and Alcohol Abuse, 15*(2), 153-172.

O'Nell, T. D., & Mitchell, C. M. (1996). Alcohol use among American Indian adolescents: The role of culture in pathological drinking. *Social Science and Medicine, 42*(4), 565-578.

The authors discuss the need for a model of adolescent alcohol use that takes into account cultural factors. Findings suggest that American Indian youth view teen drinking as pathological when specific cultural values are violated, such as generosity, modesty, or family honor.

Pharris, M. D., Resnick, M. D., & Blum, R. W. (1997). Protecting against hopelessness and suicidality in sexually abused American Indian adolescents. *Journal of Adolescent Health, 21*(6), 400-406.

This is a discussion of factors that mitigate against the negative effects of child sexual abuse.

Potthoffer, S. J., Bearinger, L. H., Skay, C. L., Cassuto, N., Blum, R. W., & Resnick, M. D. (1998). Dimensions of risk behaviors among American Indian youth. *Archives of Pediatric and Adolescent Medicine, 152*(2), 157-163.

A 162 item survey looking at 30 risk behaviors was administered in over 200 reservation schools to youth in grades 7-20 representing 50 tribes. Findings are from the total sample of 7,687 respondents.

Quinlan, K. P., Wallace, L. J., Furner, S. E., Brewer, R. D., Bolen, J., & Schieber, R. A. (1998). Motor vehicle related injuries among American Indian and Alaskan Native youth, 1981-1992: Analysis of a national hospital discharge database. *Injury Prevention, 4*(4), 276-279.

Motor vehicle related injuries and hospitalizations declined over this period of time in this population. The authors suggest that passing and enforcing tribal laws could further reduce serious injuries and fatalities.

Robin, R. W., Chester, B., Rasmuseen, J. K., Jaranson, J. M., & Goldman, D. (1997). Prevalence, characteristics and impact of childhood sexual abuse in a Southwestern American Indian tribe. *Child Abuse and Neglect, 21*(8), 769-787.

Rolland, A., Gilchrist, L. D., & Miramontez, A. (1987). Group treatment for sexually abused American Indian adolescents. *Social Work with Groups, 10*(4), 21-32.

Saewyc, E. M., Skay, C. L., Bearinger, L. H., Blum, R. W., & Resnick, M. D. (1998). Sexual orientation, sexual behavior, and pregnancy among American Indian adolescents. *Journal of Adolescent Health, 23*(4), 238-247.

In this sample of over 2,000 males and 1,700 females, American Indian adolescents had higher rates of pregnancy than did other groups of teens, as well as higher numbers who identify as gay, lesbian, or bisexual.

Sage, G. P., & Burns, G. L. (1993). Attributional antecedents of alcohol use in American Indian and Euroamerican adolescents. *American Indian and Alaska Native Mental Health Research, 5*(2), 46-56.

The authors discover that American Indian youth have different explanations than do white majority youth for their use of alcohol.

Sandler, L. (1995). From desert to garden: Reconnecting disconnected youth. *Educational Leadership, 52*(8), 14-16.

A project to create a traditional Yaqui garden served to provide at-risk teens opportunities to develop basic skills and preparation for employment.

Schafer, J. R., & McIlwaine, B. D. (1992). Investigating child sexual abuse in the American Indian community. *American Indian Quarterly, 16*(2), 157-167.

Schinke, S. P., Orlandi, M. A., Botvin, G. J., Gilchrist, L., Trimble, J. E., & Locklear, V. S. (1988). Preventing substance abuse among American Indian adolescents: A bicultural competence skills approach. *Journal of Counseling Psychology, 35*(1), 87-90.

Swaim, R. C., Oetting, E. R., Thurman, P. J., Beauvais, F., & Edwards, R. W. (1993). American Indian adolescent drug use and socialization characteristics: A cross-cultural comparison. *Journal of Cross-Cultural Psychology, 24*(1), 53-71.

Tempest, P., & Skipper, B. (1988). Norms for the Weschler Intelligence Scale for Children: Revised for Navajo students. *Diagnostique, 13*(2), 123-129.

Thousand, J., Rosenberg, R., Bishop, D., & Villa, R. (1997). The evolution of secondary inclusion. *Remedial and Special Education, 18*(5), 270-284.

The authors explain how using native culture can help develop high schools that are inclusive of adolescents with learning differences.

Thurman, P. J., & Green, V. A. (1997). American Indian adolescent inhalant use. *American Indian and Alaska Native Mental Health Research, 8*(1), 24-40.

Tuthill, N. M., & Wall, S. (1983). *Enhancing permanency outcome for Indian children under tribal jurisdiction: training curriculum.* Albuquerque, NM: American Indian Law Center.

Vandenberg, J., & Minto, B. A. (1987). Alaska Native youth: A new approach to serving emotionally disturbed children and youth. *Children Today, 16*(5), 15-18.

Watchman, D. (1982). *Indian Child Welfare: Working together to make it work-A report on demonstration training for tribal and state agency workers.* Seattle, WA: Northwest Regional Child Welfare Training Center.

Weaver, H. N. (1996). Social work with American Indian youth using the orthogonal model of cultural identification. *Families in Society: The Journal of Contemporary Human Services, 77*(2), 98-107.

Weaver, H. N. (1999). Health concerns for Native American youth: A culturally grounded approach to health promotion. *Journal of Human Behavior in the Social Environment, 2*(1/2), 127-143.

What will Jeri do? American Indian youth and inhalant abuse [VHS]. (1991). (Available from the University of New Mexico Center for Indian Youth Program Development, Albuquerque, NM.)

> **A teen girl is tempted to use inhalants by her friends. Her grandfather discusses traditional attitudes toward use of substances, and a physician discusses physical effects. This film is designed to encourage discussion.**

Wright, L., Mercer, S., Mullin, S., Thurston, K., & Harned, A. J. (1994). Differences between American Indian and non-Indian children referred for psychological services. *American Indian and Alaska Native Mental Health Research, 5*(3), 45-51.

> **The authors state that American Indian children are exposed to greater physical, health, and social risks that impact psychological development than are other children.**

Young, T. J., & French. L. A. (1997). Homicide rates among Native American children: The status integration hypothesis. *Adolescence, 32*(125), 57-59.

> **The authors find that analysis of data for all IHS service areas supported the hypothesis of status integration.**

Zimmerman, M. A., Ramirez-Valles, J., Washienki, K. M., Walter, B., & Dyer, S. (1996). The development of a measure of enculturation for Native American youth. *American Journal of Community Psychology, 24*(2), 295-310.

> **This discussion is based on a study of 120 young native people. The authors address identity issues and challenges faced by these American Indian youngsters.**

ADMINISTRATION, MANAGEMENT, AND SUPERVISION

Brown, E. F. (1986). *Defining-entry level competencies for public welfare workers serving Indian communities.* Manuscript submitted by Arizona State University School of Social Work to DHHS.

MacEachron, A. E. (1994). Supervision in tribal and state child welfare agencies: Professionalization, responsibilities, training needs, and satisfaction. *Child Welfare, 73*(2), 117-128.

White, J. (1998). Supervision and management of American Indian social and human services workers. In A. Daley (Ed.), *Workplace diversity: Issues and perspectives* (pp. 36-44). Washington, DC: NASW Press.

> **Part of the article was not included due to editorial oversight, but the article contains some initial ideas and insights for supervisors working with American Indian staff.**

AGING

Betts, N. M., & Crase, C. (1986). Nutrient intake of urban elderly American Indians. *Journal of Nutrition for the Elderly, 1*(5), 11-18.

Chapelski, E. E., Lichtenberg, P. A., Dwyer, J. W., Youngblade, L. M., & Tsai, P. F. (1997). Morbidity and co-morbidity among Great Lakes American Indians: Predictors of functional ability. *Gerontologist, 37*(5), 588-597.

> **The authors present a methodology to identify and predict degree of disability among American Indian elders.**

Hepburn, K., & Reed, R. (1995). Ethical and clinical issues with Native American elders: End-of-life decision making. *Clinics in Geriatric Medicine, 11*(1), 97-111.

> **The authors give culturally aware guidelines for discussing dying with terminally ill indigenous patients and their families.**

Hudson, M. F., Armachain, W. D., Beasley, C. M., & Carolson, J. R. (1998). Elder abuse: Two Native American views. *Gerontologist, 38*(5), 538-548.

Johnson, F. L., Cook, E., Foxall, M., Kelleher, E., Kentapp, E. (1984). Life satisfaction of the elderly American Indian. *White Cloud Journal of American Indian Mental Health, 7*(3), 3-13.

Kaufmann, C., & Barolin, G. S. (1995). Psychorehabilitation aspects in older age groups. *Experimental Gerontology, 30*(3/4), 423-430.

> **The authors explain how cultural traditions can be useful in treating older native persons. It is possible to incorporate these into western approaches to rehabilitation.**

Kettl, P. (1998). Alaska Native suicide: Lessons for elder suicide. *International Psychogeriatrics, 10*(2), 205-211.

> **Suicide rates among Alaska Native Elders are low compared to the general population. The authors show that this appears to be a result of cultural teachings, even in times of change such as the Alaska oil boom. The authors then conclude that social factors appear to influence suicide rates, both positively and negatively.**

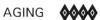

Kramer, B. J. (1992). Health and aging of urban American Indians. *Western Journal of Medicine, 157*(3), 281-285.

> Half of American Indians live off the reserve, but research on their health status is limited. Native people living in urban areas are not eligible for IHS services, but are nonetheless at high risk for many health problems. The authors identify barriers that interfere with access to health care, particularly for older persons, and demonstrate that it is possible to provide better access to services for older native people.

Kramer, B. J. (1995). American Indian families and home care: Macro social and cultural considerations. *Alaska Medicine, 37*(4), 139-141.

> The authors discuss programs to support home health care in reservation settings.

Lyman, A. J., & Edwards, M. E. (1989). Poetry: Life review for frail American Indian elderly. *Journal of Gerontological Social Work, 14*(1-2), 75-91.

Manson, S. M. (1989). Provider assumptions about long-term care in American Indian communities. *The Gerontologist, 29*(3), 355-358.

Mercer, S. O. (1996). Navajo elderly people in a reservation nursing home: Admission predictors and cultural care practices. *Social Work, 41*, 181-189.

> This article establishes culturally sensitive principles and practices for the care of older Native Americans.

Narduzzi, J. L. (1994). *Mental health among elderly Native Americans.* New York: Garland Publications.

Orr, A. L. (1993). Training outreach workers to serve American Indian elders with visual impairment and diabetes. *Journal of Visual Impairment and Blindness, 87*(9), 336-340.

> The authors discuss teaching independent living skills to mature adults. They propose ways to train health and human services workers to outreach to this population, which has significant rates of diabetes and corollary disease.

Rousseau, P. (1995). Native American elders: Health-care status. *Clinics in Geriatric Medicine, 1*(1), 83-95.

Steele, L., & Hisnanick, J. (1995). Home health care for cancer patients: Insights from the American Indian community. *Alaska Medicine, 37*(4), 127-131.

> This article is a description of a home health care program for older individuals.

Theobald, B. (1991). *Qualitative study of the meaning of aging to European American middle class and Native American participants in a senior citizens' nutrition program.* Unpublished Master's thesis, Syracuse University, NY.

ALCOHOL AND SUBSTANCE ABUSE

Abbott, P. J. (1998). Traditional and Western healing practices for alcoholism in American Indians and Alaska Natives. *Substance Use and Misuse, 33*(13), 2605-2646.

> A variety of healing practices have been used in the treatment of alcoholism among native groups, including sacred dances, sweat lodges, and talking circles. These have been combined with Western approaches, such as the use of medication to assist in withdrawal and to maintain sobriety. The authors discuss how Native communities can use both approaches to meet the needs of their people.

Albaugh, D. (1974). Peyote in the treatment of alcoholism among American Indians. *American Journal of Psychiatry, 13*(1), 1247-1250.

Are you listening? American Indian families and inhalant abuse [VHS]. (1991). (Available from the University of New Mexico, Center for Indian Youth Program Development, Albuquerque, NM.)

> This is a case study of how a child has to be hospitalized as a result of inhalant use.

Back, W. D. (1981). The ineffectiveness of alcohol prohibition on the Navajo Indian reservation. *Arizona State Law Journal, 4*(1), 925-943.

> Reservations have attempted to prohibit the sale and consumption of alcohol on tribal lands. However, the author shows that this has not proven to be an effective approach to alcohol prevention because enforcement of regulations is difficult and many communities have liquor stores just beyond reservation boundaries.

Beauvais, F. (1992). Comparison of drug use rates for reservation Indian, non-reservation Indian and Anglo youth. *American Indian and Alaska Native Mental Health Research, 5*(1), 13-31.

Beauvais, F. (1992). The consequences of drug and alcohol use for Indian youth. *American Indian and Alaska Native Mental Health Research, 5*(1), 32-37.

Beauvais, F. (1992). An integrated model for prevention and treatment of drug abuse among American Indian youth. *Journal of Addictive Diseases, 11*(3), 68-80.

Beauvais, F. (1992). Trends in Indian adolescent drug and alcohol abuse. *American Indian and Alaska Native Mental Health Research, 5*(1), 1-12.

Beauvais, F., & LaBoueff, S. (1985). Drug and alcohol intervention in American Indian communities. *International Journal of Addictions, 20*(1), 139-171.

Beauvais, F., Oetting, E. R., & Edwards, R. W. (1985a). Trends in drug use of Indian adolescents living on reservations, 1975-1983. *American Journal on Drug and Alcohol Dependence, 11*(3), 209-229.

Beauvais, F., Oetting, E. R., & Edwards, R. W. (1985b). Trends in the use of inhalants among American Indian adolescents. *White Cloud Journal of American Indian Mental Health, 3*(4), 3-11.

Canda, E. R., & Yellow Bird, M. J. (1997). Another view, cultural strengths are crucial. *Families in Society: The Journal of Contemporary Human Services, 78*(3), 248.

> The entire community is the most effective clinic. This article provides a short commentary of how cultural strengths are crucial in the development of culturally competent strategies for AOD abuse treatment.

Children of alcoholics [VHS and 16mm]. (1983). (Available from the National Film Board, Toronto, Canada)

> This film shows how alcohol affects a First Nations family in a rural community.

Debby and Sharon—Recovery [VHS]. (1985). (Available from the National Film Board of Canada, Montreal, Canada)

> This film is about First Nations women and problem drinking. Two women who are in recovery are interviewed.

Edwards, E. D., & Edwards, M. E. (1988). Alcoholism prevention/treatment and Native American youth: A community approach. *The Journal of Drug Issues, 18*(1), 103-114.

> This article discusses a community-based approach to the prevention and treatment of alcohol abuse in native young people.

French, L. (1990). Substance abuse treatment among American Indian children. *Alcoholism Treatment Quarterly, 7*(2), 63-76.

French, L. A., & Hornbuckle, J. (1979). Indian stress and violence: A psycho-cultural perspective. *Journal of Alcohol and Drug Education, 25*(1), 36-43.

French, L. A., & Hornmbuckle, J. (1980). Alcoholism among Native Americans: An analysis. *Social Work, 25*, 275-280.

Garcia-Andrade, G., Wall, T. L., & Ehlers, C. L. (1996). Alcohol expectancies in a Native American population. *Alcoholism, Clinical and Experimental Research, 20*(8), 1438-1441.

> The authors show that, as with other populations, Native American drinking patterns are related to alcohol expectancies.

Gilchrist, L., Schinke, S. P., Trimble, J. E., & Cvetkovich, G. (1987). Skills enhancement to prevent substance abuse among American Indian adolescents. *International Journal of the Addictions, 22*(9), 869-879.

Goldstein, G. S., Oetting, E. R., & Edwards, R. (1979). Drug use among Native American young adults. *International Journal of the Addictions, 14*(1), 855-869.

> This article may be useful in comparing rates of drug use at the time with drug use at later dates.

Guiterres, S. E., Russo, N. F., & Urbanski, L. (1994). Sociocultural and psychological factors in American Indian drug use: Implications for treatment. *International Journal of the Addictions, 29*(4), 1761-1786.

Characteristics of male and female drug abusers and implications for prevention and treatment are explored.

Hall, R. L. (1986). Alcohol treatment in American Indian populations: An indigenous treatment modality compared with traditional approaches. In T. F. Baber (Ed.), *Alcohol and culture: Comparative perspectives from Europe and America* (pp. 168-177). New York: New York Academy of Sciences.

One of the continuing issues in treatment of alcohol and other substance abuse among American Indians is determining the success of treatment approaches which utilize cultural traditions and ceremonies. This article looks at typical treatment approaches and at a program which is based on native traditions and culture.

Hassin, J. (1996). After substance abuse treatment, then what? *American Rehabilitation, 22*(2), 12-19.

This article describes an approach to providing transitional services from treatment setting to community.

Hill, T. W. (1980). Life styles and drinking patterns of urban Indians. *Journal of Drug Issues, 3*(2), 257-272.

Jilek-Aall, J. (1981). Acculturation, alcoholism and Indian-style Alcoholics Anonymous. *Journal of Studies on Alcohol, 42*(1), 143-158.

Kunitz, S. J., Levy, J. E., McCloskey, J., & Gabriel, K. R. (1998). Alcohol dependence and domestic violence sequelae of abuse and conduct disorder in childhood. *Child Abuse and Neglect, 22*(11), 1079-1091, 127-135.

Since there is a correlation between alcohol dependence, domestic violence, and the behavior of children, the treatment of women is particularly crucial in intervening in the cycle of abuse and behavioral dysfunction. This article explains approaches and attitudes which help native women toward recovery within a cultural context.

Kvigne, V. L., Bull, L. B., Welty, T. K., Leonardson, G. R., & Lacina, L. (1998). Relationship of prenatal alcohol use with maternal and prenatal factors in American Indian women. *Social Biology, 45*(3/4), 214-222.

The authors explain that patterns of prenatal drinking and access to transportation correlate with other factors that place the preborn and infant child at risk.

Lobb, M. L., & Watts, T. D. (1989). *Native American youth and alcohol: An annotated bibliography.* Westport, CT: Greenwood.

Mail, P. D. (1980). American Indian drinking behavior: Some possible causes and solutions. *Journal of Alcohol and Drug Education, 26*(1), 28-39.

Mail, P. D. (1985). Closing the circle: A prevention model for Indian communities with alcohol problems. *IHS Primary Care Provider, 10*(1), 2-5.

Mail, P. D., & Johnson, S. (1993). Boozing, sniffing, and toking: An overview of the past, present, and future of substance abuse by American Indians. *American Indian and Alaska Native Mental Health Research, 5*(2), 1-33.

Maracle, B. (1994). *Crazywater: Native voices on addiction and recovery.* Toronto, Canada: Penguin Books.

May, P. A. (1986). Alcohol and drug misuse prevention programs for American Indians: Needs and opportunities. *Journal of Studies on Alcoholism, 47*(3), 187-195.

May, P. A. (1992). Alcohol policy considerations for Indian reservations and border town communities. *American Indian and Alaska Native Mental Health Research, 4*(3), 5-59.

> **The author examines the issues surrounding the fact that although reservations may have policies prohibiting the sale and distribution of alcoholic beverages, residents can easily obtain these in adjacent communities. Indeed, the author points out, one often sees numerous liquor stores at the reservation borders.**

McBride, D. C., & Page, J. B. (1980). Adolescent Indian substance abuse: Ecological and socio-cultural factors. *Youth and Society, 11*(4), 475-492.

Moncher, M. S., Holden, G. W., & Rimble, G. E. (1990). Substance abuse among Native American youth. *Journal of Consulting and Clinical Psychology, 58*(4), 408-415.

Moran, J. (1995). Culturally sensitive alcohol-prevention research in ethnic communities. In P. Langton (Ed.), *The challenge of participatory research: Preventing alcohol-related problems in ethnic communities* (pp. 43-56). Washington, DC: National Institute on Alcohol Abuse and Alcoholism Center for Substance Abuse Treatment.

Moran, J., & May, P. A. (1995). American Indians. In J. Phillelo & F. L. Brisbane (Eds.), *Cultural competence for social workers: A guide for alcohol and other drug abuse prevention professionals working with ethnic/racial communities* (DHS # SMA 95-3075). Washington, DC: U.S. Department of Health and Human Services, Public Health Services, SAMHSA.

Murphy, S. (1984). Substance abuse and the Native American student. *Journal of Drug Education, 14*(4), 315-321.

Native American Educational Services College Library and Archives. (1997). *Alcohol and drug abuse bibliography* [On-line]. Available: *http://naes.indian.com/alcohol.html.*

> **This is an 11 page bibliography of alcohol and drug abuse, with many of the items relevant to urban Indian communities.**

Nofz, M. P. (1988). Alcohol abuse and the culturally marginal American Indian. *Social Casework, 69*(2), 67-73.

Oetting, E. R., Beauvais, F., & Edwards, R. (1988). Alcohol and Indian youth: Social and psychological correlates and prevention. *The Journal of Drug Issues, 18*(1), 87-101.

Oetting, E. R., Edwards, R., Goldstein, G. S., & Garcia-Mason, V. (1980). Drug use among adolescents of five southwestern Native American tribes. *International Journal of Addictions, 15*(3), 439-445.

O'Nell, T. D. (1992/1993). Feeling worthless: An investigation of depression and problem drinking at the Flathead reservation. *Culture, Medicine and Psychiatry, 16*(4), 447-469.

> **The author focuses on cultural factors including the disruption of social bonds and cultural demoralization that contribute to substance abuse, depression, and suicidality.**

Parker, L. (1990). The missing component in substance abuse prevention efforts: A Native American example. *Contemporary Drug Problems, 74*(6), 251-270.

Pascarosa, P., & Futterman, S. (1976). Ethnopyschedelic therapy for alcoholics: Observations on the peyote ritual of the Native American church. *Journal of Psychedelic Drugs, 8*(3), 215-221.

> **This article demonstrates the interest in the use of hallucinogens in alcohol treatment that marked the 1960s and 1970s. The Native American Church is a recognized religious body with traditions that date back hundreds, possibly thousands, of years, including the use of peyote. There are definite criteria for the use of this substance in this spiritual context. The authors explore ways in which peyote and similar hallucinogens can be used in the treatment of alcoholics.**

Popham, R. E. (1979). Psychocultural barriers to successful alcoholism therapy in an American Indian patient. *Journal of Studies on Alcoholism, 40*(7), 656-676.

Public Health Service (1991). *Prevention resource guide: American Indians and Native Alaskans.* (DHHS Publication No. ADM 91-1802). Washington, DC: National Clearinghouse for Drug and Alcohol Information.

Robin, C. W., Long, J. C., Rasmussen, J. K., Albaugh, B., & Goldman, D. (1998). Relationship of binge drinking to alcohol dependence, other psychiatric disorders and behavioral problems in an American Indian tribe. *Alcohol, Clinical and Experimental Research, 22*(2), 518-523.

> **In this sample of 582 American Indians, the authors explore the relationship between binge drinking and alcohol dependency. They find a positive association, as well as an association with other psychiatric disorders and violent behavior.**

Robin, R. W., Chester, B., Rasmussen, J. K., Jaranson, J. J., & Goldman, D. (1997). Factors influencing utilization of mental health and substance abuse services by American Indian men and women. *Psychiatric Services, 48*(6), 826-832.

> **The authors find a correlation between sex, psychiatric diagnosis, childhood sexual abuse, and the use of mental health and substance abuse treatment services in this sample of 600.**

Sage, G., & Burns, G. L. (1993). Attributional antecedents of alcohol use in American Indian and Euroamerican adolescents. *American Indian and Alaska Native Mental Health Research, 5*(2), 46-56.

Schinke, S. (1985). Preventing substance abuse with American Indian youth. *Social Casework, 66*(5), 213-217.

Schinke, S. P., Botvin, G. J., Trimble, J. E., Orlandi, M. A., Gilchrist, L. D., & Locklear, V. S. (1988). Preventing substance abuse among American Indian adolescents: A bicultural competence skills approach. *Journal of Counseling Psychology, 35*(1), 87-90.

Schinke, S. P., Gilchrist, L. D., Schilling, R. F. II, Walker, R. D., Kirkham, M. A., Bobo, J. K., Trimble, J. E., Cvetkovich, G. T., & Richardson, S. S. (1985). Strategies for preventing substance abuse with American Indian youth. *White Cloud Journal of American Indian Health, 3*(4). Pages are not numbered.

Schinke, S. P., Moncher, M. S., Holden, G. W., Botvin, G. J., & Orlandi, M. A. (1989). American Indian youth and substance abuse: Tobacco use problems, risk factors, and preventive interventions. *Health Education Research, 4*(1), 137-144.

Soul spirit [VHS]. (1989). (Available from Anishnawbe Health Center, Toronto, Canada)

An elder talks about his alcoholism, recovery, and factors in First Nations culture that help toward recovery.

Spicer, P. (1997). Toward a dysfunctional anthropology of drinking: Ambivalence and the American Indian experience with alcohol. *Medical Anthropology Quarterly, 11*(3), 306-323.

Although American Indian drinkers are aware of the effect heavy drinking has on their functioning, they continue to use alcohol. This article proposes possible explanations.

Swaim, R. C., Oetting, E. R., Thurman, P. J., Beauvais, F., & Edwards, R. (1993). American Indian adolescent drug use and socialization characteristics: A cross-cultural comparison. *Journal of Counseling Psychology, 24*(2), 53-70.

Thomas, R. (1981). The history of North American Indian alcohol use as a community based phenomena. *Journal of Studies on Alcohol, (*Suppl. *9)*, 29-39.

Trimble, J. E. (1992). A cognitive-behavioral approach to drug prevention and intervention with American Indian youth. In L. A. Vargas & J. D. Koss-Chioino (Eds.), *Working with culture: Psychotherapuetic interventions with ethnic minority children and adolescents* (pp. 246-275). San Francisco: Jossey-Bass.

Walker, R. D., Lambert, M. D., Walker, P. S., & Kivlaham, D. R. (1992/1993). Treatment implications of comorbid psychopathology in American Indian and Alaska Natives. *Culture, Medicine and Psychiatry, 16*(4), 555-572.

Barriers to treatment, including lack of appropriate interventions, may interfere with American Indian populations' use of available treatment resources. The article discusses this issue and also includes information about Western and traditional approaches to treatment.

Walker, R. D., Lambert, M. D., Walker, P. S., Kivlahan, D. R., Donovan, D. M., & Howard, M. O. (1996). Alcohol abuse in American Indian adolescents and women: A longitudinal study for assessment and risk evaluation. *American Indian and Alaska Native Mental Health Research, 7*(1), 1-47.

This is an empirical study of over 500 native women and 250 native youth in a longitudinal study over a ten-year period. The article examines alcohol and drug use and mental health status in a community of urban native people.

Watts, T. D., & Lewis, R. G. (1988). Alcoholism and Native American youth: An overview. *The Journal of Drug Issues, 18*(1), 69-86.

Young, T. J. (1987). Inhalant use among American Indian youth. *Child Psychiatry and Human Development, 18*(3), 36-45.

CHILD WELFARE: INDIAN CHILD WELFARE ACT

Atwood, B. A. (1989). Fighting over Indian children: The uses and abuses of jurisdictional ambiguity. *UCLA Law Review, 36*(6), 1051-1108.

Bennett, M. (1993). Native American children: Caught in the web of the Indian Child Welfare Act. *Hamline Law Review 16*(3), 953-973.

Blanchard, E., & Barch, R. L. (1980). What is best for tribal children? *Social Work, 25*, 350-357.

> This was written at the time of debate by non-Indians about the Indian Child Welfare Act. The author defends the Indian Child Welfare Act in a response to an article in the same issue by R. S. Fishler entitled "Protecting American Indian children." Fishler argued that the Indian Child Welfare Act did not adequately protect native children.

Canda, E. R., Carrizosa, S., & Yellow Bird, M. (1995). *Culturally competent child welfare practice: A training curriculum* (3rd ed.) [Manual]. (Available from the Kansas Department of SRS under Title IV-E, KS)

> This manual provides a training curriculum for cultural competence for child welfare workers. It is intended to assist workers to improve their skills to implement culturally competent work with children and families.

Children of Wind River [U-matic television program]. (1989). (Available from Wyoming Public Television, Riverton, WY)

> Tribal leaders talk about teen suicide, poverty, and alcohol abuse on the reservation.

Circle of life [VHS]. (1990). (Available from Leech Lake Reservation, Health Division, Cass Lake, MN)

> Teens discuss and give advice about substance abuse, teen pregnancy and parenting, and violence in relationships.

Cross Cultural Issues and Risk Assessment and *Cross Cultural Issues in Out -Of-Home Care* [VHS, two tapes]. (1991). (Available from Northwest Indian Child Welfare Association, Portland, OR)

> The videos examine how cultural factors are involved in child placement and temporary care, and they stress that social workers need to be aware of misunderstandings that can lead to poor placement decisions. Additionally, the videos explain that risk assessment tools designed for use with majority children are often not appropriate for use with American Indian families. The Indian Child Welfare Act is also discussed.

Foerster, L. M. (1974). Open education and Native American values. *Educational Leadership, 32*(1), 41-45.

> **The author suggests that open classrooms are compatible with traditional Native American values and ways of life.**

Foerster, L. M. (1977). Trends in early childhood education for Native American pupils. *Educational Leadership, 34*(5), 373-378.

Goldstein, J., & Goldstein, S. (1996). "Put yourself in the skin of the child," she said. *Psychoanalytic Study of the Child, 51*, 46-55.

> **This is a case of two American Indian children adopted by a non-Indian family that came before the U.S. Supreme Court and an Indian Tribal Court. The authors discuss issues of transcultural adoption and contested placements.**

Gonzalez-Santin, E. (n.d.). *The White Mountain child protection service training curriculum: Nohwii chaghashe baa da gontzaa (protect our Apache children)* [Training Manual]. White River, AZ: White Mountain Apache Tribe (Available from Arizona State University, Tempe, School of Social Work).

> **This is a comprehensive training manual providing information on native communities, lifestyles, medical and sociological issues including risk factors for abuse, legal issues in federal and tribal law, child protective service procedures and protocols, tribal community practice, healing and wellness in an indigenous context, and teaching tools and tips for trainers.**

Goodluck, C. (1975). Indian adoption project. *Smith College for Social Work Journal, 1*(2), 7-10.

Goodluck, C. (1975). Indian adoption project. *Smith College for Social Work Journal, 2*(1), 1-4.

Goodluck, C. (1993). Social services with Native Americans: Current status of the Indian Child Welfare Act. In H. P. McAdoo (Ed.), *Family ethnicity: Strength in diversity* (pp. 217-226). Newbury Park, CA: Sage.

Goodluck, C. (1997). *Tribal-state child welfare project: Final report.* Englewood, CO: National Resource Center on Child Abuse and Neglect, American Humane Association, Children's Division.

Goodluck, C., & Brown, M. E. (1980). *Decision-making regarding American Indian children in foster care.* Phoenix, AZ: Jewish Family and Children's Services.

Goodluck, C., & Eckstein, F. (1977). American Indian adoption program. *Adoption Report, 2*(2), 23-35.

Goodluck, C., & Eckstein, F. (1978). American Indian adoption program: An ethnic approach to child welfare. *White Cloud Journal of American Indian Health, 1*(1), 4-6.

Goodluck, C., & Martin. S. (1991). *Adoption sourcebook.* Denver, CO: University of Denver, Family Resource Center, Region VIII.

Goodluck, C., & Short, D. (1980). Working with American Indian parents: A cultural approach. *Social Casework, 61*(8), 472-475.

Grandboise, G. H. (1980). *Indian child welfare: A beginning.* Omaha, NE: University of Nebraska, Omaha, School of Social Work.

Gray, E., & Cosgrove, J. (1985). Ethnocentric perception of child rearing practices in protective services. *Child Abuse and Neglect, 9*(2), 386-396.

Protective services workers are not always aware of cultural differences in raising children, and the authors contend that this leads to institutional abuse of minority families. Child-rearing practices of six groups, including Blackfeet, are discussed.

Horesji, C., & Craig, B. (1992). Reactions by Native American parents to child protection agencies: Cultural and community factors. *Child Welfare, 71*(4), 329.

The authors explain how cultural experiences of oppression make it difficult for native parents to provide appropriate parenting or accept help from government staff and organizations.

Ishisaka, H. (1978). American Indians and foster care: Cultural factors and separation. *Child Welfare, 57*(5), 299-306.

Johnson, B. B. (1981). The Indian Child Welfare Act of 1978: Implications for practice. *Child Welfare, 60*(7), 435-446.

Kessel, J. A., & Robbins, S. P. (1984). The Indian Child Welfare Act: Dilemmas and needs. *Child Welfare, 63*(3), 225-232.

McMahon, A., & Gullerud, E. N. (1995). Native American agencies for Native American children: Fulfilling the promise of the Indian Child Welfare Act. *Journal of Sociology and Social Welfare, 22*(1), 87-98.

Myers, J. A. (Ed.). (1981). *They are young once but Indian forever: A summary and analysis of investigative hearings on Indian Child welfare, April, 1980.* Oakland, CA: American Indian Lawyer Training Program.

Nybell, L. M. (1985). *A sourcebook in child welfare: Serving American Indian families and children.* Ann Arbor, MI: National Child Welfare Training Center, the University of Michigan, School of Social Work.

Citations from 1969 through 1984 for those interested in cultural issues relevant to social work practice with native families and the Indian Child Welfare Act.

Our children are our future [Film]. (1982). (Available from Direction Films, Toronto, Canada)

This work presents issues related to First Nations children placed in non-native homes.

Palmer, S., & Cooke, W. (1996). Understanding and countering racism in First Nations children in out-of-home care. *Child Welfare, 75*(6), 709-725.

Canadian native children are often placed with non-natives and encounter racism in these homes. This article discusses ways to help First Nations people retain their own children and combat racism in foster care.

Renner, J. R. (1992). The Indian Child Welfare Act and equal protection limitations on the federal power over Indian affairs. *American Indian Law Review, 17*(1), 129-174.

Tuthill, N. M., & Wall, S. (1983). *Enhancing permanency outcome for Indian children under the Tribal Court jurisdiction.* Albuquerque, NM: American Indian Law Center.

Wares, D. M., Wedel, K. R., Rosenthal, J. A., & Dobrec, A. (1994). Indian child welfare: A multicultural challenge. *Journal of Multicultural Social Work, 3*(3), 1-15.

Watchman, D. (1982). *Indian child welfare: Working together to make it work—A report on demonstration training for tribal and state agency workers.* Seattle, WA: Northwest Regional Child Welfare Training Center, University of Washington, School of Social Work (Available from National Child Welfare Training Center, University of Michigan, School of Social Work, 1080 S. University, Ann Arbor, MI 48109-1106).

Weaver, H. N., & White, B. J. (1999). Protecting the future of indigenous children and nations: An examination of the Indian Child Welfare Act. *Journal of Health and Social Policy, 10*(4), 35-50.

CULTURE, VALUES, AND IDENTITY

Alberta, A. (1986). *He' ho niyo' de: No'—That's what it was like.* Lakawanne, NY: Bebco Enterprises.

Allen, P. (1986). *The sacred hoop: Recovering the feminine in American Indian traditions.* Boston: Beacon Press.

Allen, P. (1991). *Grandmothers of the light: A medicine woman's source book.* Boston: Beacon Press.

Andrews, L. V. (1981). *Medicine woman.* San Francisco: Harper and Row.

Angell, B. (2000). Cultural resilience in North American Indian First Nations: The story of Little Turtle [On-line]. *Critical Social Work, 1*(1). Available: *http://core/ecu.edu/socw/csw/ 00_1cultural_ang.html*

Angell, G. B. (1997). Madness in the family: The "windigo." *Journal of Family Social Work, 2*(2), 179-196.

> **This article examines how northeastern native peoples of the Alquonqian group use the concept of the windigo to explain why bad things happen. This concept is a means of empowerment of the person as well as a way to separate the individual from the problem.**

Baird, R. (1996). Going Indian: Discovery, adoption and renaming toward a 'true American,' from Deerslayer to Dances with Wolves. In S. E. Bird (Ed.), *Dressing in feathers: The construction of the Indian in American popular culture* (pp. 195-209). Boulder,CO: Westview Press.

Barthwell, A. Hewitt, W., & Jilson, I. (1988). An introduction to ethnic and cultural diversity. *Pediatric Clinics of North America, 42*(2), 431-451.

Bird, E. S. (1999). Gendered construction of the American Indian in popular media. *Journal of Communications, 49*(3), 61-62.

Bordewich, F. M. (1996). *Killing the White Man's Indian: Reinventing Native Americans at the end of the twentieth century.* New York: Doubleday.

Bowman, B. J. (1996). Cross-cultural validation of Antonovsky's Sense of Coherence Scale. *Journal of Clinical Psychology, 52*(5), 547-549.

> This study supports Antonovsky's hypothesis that a sense of coherence is vital to management of stress and psychological and physical well-being. He further suggests that this is true across cultures.

Brave Heart, M. Y., & DeBruyn, L. M. (1998). The American Indian holocaust: Healing historical unresolved grief. *American Indian and Alaska Native Mental Health Research, 8*(2), 56-78.

> The impact of losses resulting from European contact include unresolved grief across generations which, the authors contend, contributes to high rates of social pathology among native peoples. The authors draw upon holocaust literature and suggest interventions for healing this trauma.

Brizinski, P. M. (1993). The summer meddler: The image of the anthropologist as tool for indigenous formulations of culture. In N. Dyck & J. B. Waldram (Eds.), *Anthropology, public policy, and native peoples in Canada.* Montreal, Canada: McGill-Queen's University Press.

Brown. D. (1970). *Bury my heart at Wounded Knee.* New York: Henry Holt.

Bureau of the Census. (1993). *We the ... First Americans.* Washington, DC: Author.

Cahn, E. S. (1970). *Our brother's keeper: The Indian in White America.* Washington, DC: New Community Press.

Churchill, W. (1994). *Indians are us? Culture and genocide in Native North America.* Monroe, ME: Common Courage Press.

Churchill, W. (1998). *Fantasies of the master race: Literature, cinema and the colonization of American Indians.* San Francisco, CA: City Lights Books.

> This was issued in an earlier edition by Common Courage Press, Monroe, ME, in 1992.

Communicating with Native American patients [VHS]. (1988). (Available from Native American Research Training Center, Tuscon, AZ)

> A Navajo health care provider discusses communication issues, ways to establish a relationship, how to encourage compliance, the role of interpreters, and the use of native healers.

Deloria, V., Jr. (1995). *Red earth, white lies: Native Americans and the myth of scientific fact.* New York: Scribner.

Dene Family [VHS]. (n.d.). (Available from Dr. Otto Schaefer Resource Center, Department of Health, Government of the Northwest Territories, Yellowknife, Canada)

> This short film depicts the daily life of a Dene family in an isolated rural village.

Dooling, D. (Ed.). (1992). *The sons of the wind: The sacred stories of the Lakota.* San Francisco: Harper Collins.

Dorris, M. (1989). *The broken cord.* New York: Harper & Row.

DuBray, W. H. (1985). American Indian values: Critical factor in casework. *Social Casework, 66*(1), 30-37.

Effects of heritage, progress, and stereotypes on Indian health professionals [VHS]. (1984). (Available from the John Vaughan Library, Learning Resources Center, Northeastern State University, 711 N. Grand, Tahlequah, OK 74464)

This is a film of a speech given at a symposium on the American Indian, at the Division of Social Sciences of Northeastern State University.

Goodluck, C. (1990). Native American ideas in helping and healing: Diversity in action. *Smith College School for Social Work Journal. 60*(3), 43-47.

Goodluck, C. (1993). Social services with Native Americans: Current status of the Indian Child Welfare Act. In H. P. McAdoo (Ed.), *Family ethnicity: Strength in diversity* (pp. 217 – 226). Newbury Park, CA: Sage.

The author discusses cultural variables that affect compliance with this law.

Good Tracks, J. G. (1973). Native American non-interference. *Social Work, 19,* 30-35.

Grandboise, G. H., & Schadt, D. (1994). Indian identification and alienation in an urban community. *Psychological Reports, 74*(1), 211-216.

Green, J. W. (1995). American Indians in a new world. In J. W. Green (Ed.), *Cultural awareness in the human services: A multi-ethnic approach* (pp. 95-116). Boston: Allyn and Bacon.

The chapter on American Indians provides an overview of history, policy, and special challenges facing social workers serving native communities. There is a useful table demonstrating cultural contrasts between majortiy culture and indigenous cultures.

Griffin-Pearce, T. (1997). When I am lonely the mountains call me: The impact of sacred geography on Navajo psychological well-being. *American Indian and Alaska Native Mental Health Research, 7*(3), 1-10.

The author explores emotional ties to land and the psychological dislocation which follows geographic relocation for traditional peoples. Spirituality and land are inextricably intertwined in traditional culture.

Jaimes, M. A. (Ed.). (1992). *The state of Native America: Genocide, colonization, and resistance.* Boston: South End Press.

Lame Deer, A., & Erdoes, R. (1992). *Gifts of power: The life and teachings of a Lakota medicine man.* Santa Fe, NM: Bear and Company.

Lame Deer, J., & Erdoes, R. (1972). *Lame Deer: seeker of visions.* New York: Washington Square Press.

Lowie, R. H. (1954). *Indians of the plains.* Lincoln, NE: University of Nebraska Press.

Mathiessen, P. (1991). *In the spirit of Crazy Horse.* New York; Viking Penguin.

Nabokov, P. (1991). *Native American testimony: A chronicle of Indian-White relations from prophecy to the present, 1492-1992.* New York: Penguin.

Neidhardt, J. (1932). *Black Elk speaks.* New York: William Morrow.

Ortiz, A. (1969). *The Tewa world: Space, time, being and becoming in a Pueblo society.* Chicago: University of Chicago Press.

Owens, L. (1998). *Mixedblood messages: Literature, film, family, place* (American Indian Literature and Critical Studies Series, Vol. 26). Norman, OK: University of Oklahoma Press.

Pierotti, R., & Wildcat, D. (1997). Native tradition, evolution and creation. *Winds of Change: A Magazine for American Indian Education and Opportunity, 12*(2), 70-73.

The authors contend that Native American survival depends on rejecting western paradigms of thought.

Power, S. (1994). *The grass dancer.* New York: Putnam.

Red Horse, J., & Red Horse, Y. (1981). *A cultural network model: Perspectives from an urban-American Indian youth project.* (ERIC Document Reproduction Service No. ED 248 997)

A program for adolescent girls in Minneapolis shows how extended family systems can be used in a cultural model network using tribal and traditional values orientations.

Ross, E. B. (1976). Indian languages. *American Education, 12*(7), 10-14.

The author describes a Wisconsin project to standardize writing and materials for instruction in five native languages.

Sanchez, T. R., Plawecki, J. A., & Plawecki, H. M. (1996). The delivery of culturally sensitive health care to Native Americans. *Journal of Holistic Nursing, 14*(4), 295-307.

When the practitioner understands cultural beliefs and practices it more likely health care will be readily accepted by Native American populations. Five values held by Native Americans are presented.

Sarris, G. (1993). *Keeping Slug woman alive: A holistic approach to American Indian texts.* Berkeley, CA: University of California Press.

Schiller, P. M. (1987). Biculturalism and psychosocial adjustment among Native American university students (Doctoral Dissertation, 1987) *Dissertation Abstracts International, 48* (6-A), 1542.

Shively, J. E. (1992). Cowboys and Indians: Perceptions of Western films among American Indians and Anglos. *American Sociological Review, 57*(6), 725-734.

The author looks at the ways minorities interpret central myths of the majority culture and how people make use of cultural materials. American Indian and non-Indian audiences see different meanings in the same film.

Wallace, A. (1972). *The death and rebirth of the Seneca.* New York: Random House.

Weaver, H. N. (1997). Which canoe are you in? A view from a First Nations person. *Reflections: Narratives of Professional Helping, A Journal for the Helping Professions, 4*(3), 12-17.

Weaver, H. N. (2000). Culture and professional education: The experiences of Native American social workers. *Journal of Social Work Education, 36*, 415-429.

Weaver, H. N. (in press). Activism and American Indian issues: Opportunities and roles for social workers. *Journal of Progressive Human Services.*

Weaver, H. N., & Yellow Horse Brave Heart, M. (1999). Examining two facets of American Indian identity: Exposure to other cultures and the influence of historical trauma. *Journal of Human Behavior in the Social Environment, 2*(1/2), 19-33.

We look, you look: Perspectives on acculturation [VHS]. (1989). (Available from the Native American Research and Training Center, Tucson, AZ)

> **This film presents American Indian values and beliefs about time, death, religion, and life.**

Wilkinson, C. (1987). *American Indians, time, and the law.* New Haven, CT: Yale University Press.

Williams, E. E., & Ellison, F. (1992). Culturally informed social work practice with American Indian clients: Guidelines for non-Indian social workers. *Social Work, 41*, 147-151.

> **The authors discuss groups of American Indian peoples according to their degree of acculturation, ranging from traditional, who "live in accordance with culturally prescribed customs," to marginals "caught between traditional roots and white society," to the middle class "who are more likely to subscribe to Western society's way of life," and Pan-Indians who "struggle to re-establish lost traditions in a way that encompasses tribal variation." The authors believe that social work health and mental health interventions should be congruent with the native person's degree of acculturation and that client beliefs about health and illness should be considered. Included in this article are general guidelines for work with American Indians and a brief bibliography. This is a generic article which alerts readers to the need for cultural sensitivity and differences among tribes.**

Williams, T. C. (1976). *The reservation.* Syracuse, NY: University Press.

Wilson, E. (1991). *Apologies to the Iroquois.* Syracuse, NY: University Press. (Original work published 1959)

Wilson, T. (1992). Blood quantum: Native American mixed bloods. In M. Root (Ed.), *Racially mixed people in America* (pp. 108-125). Newbury Park, CA: Sage Publications.

> **The federal government required tribes to define the basis for tribal membership. The author discusses the concept of blood quantum as the basis for tribal enrollment and continuance on the rolls.**

Yellow Bird, M. (1995). Spirituality in First Nations story telling: A Sahnish-Hidatsa approach to narrative. *Reflections: Narratives of Professional Helping, A Journal for the Helping Professions, 1*(4), 65-72.

> Storytelling is one of the most important ways to define and give meaning to the spirituality of First Nations peoples. In this article the author shares four aspects of storytelling that support the spirituality of First Nations peoples. The narratives of the author's village attest to the pain, loss, resiliency, hope, and humanity that is found among his peoples.

Yellow Bird, M. (1998). *Invited commentary on multicultural social work education—A perspective on community practice.* Conference for Culturally Competent Social Work Education in the 21st Century. Ann Arbor, MI.

> Understanding and implementing multiculturalism and cultural competency frameworks in community social work practice curriculums are critical to social justice. This paper reviews Felix Rivera's perspectives on community practice and finds considerable agreement with his ideas.

Yellow Bird, M. (1999). Indian, American Indian, and Native Americans: Counterfeit identities. *Winds of Change: A Magazine for American Indian Education and Opportunity, 14*(1), 86.

> In this critical essay, the author argues that Indian, American Indian, and Native American are inaccurate, confusing, and colonized identities. He maintains that the continued use of these terms is oppressive and that the scholarship about First Nations peoples must be decolonized through the use of more empowering descriptors.

Yellow Bird, M. (1999). Radical, skewed, benign, and calculated: reflections on teaching diversity. *Reflections, Narratives of Professional Helping: A Journal for the Helping Professions, 4*(2), 13-22.

> This article is a narrative that shares the author's experience teaching diversity in an undergraduate social work program. First, he shares experiences teaching diversity as a Ph.D. student. Second, he discusses how teaching social work with First Nations in Canada influenced his later teaching of diversity. Third, he attempts to define diversity and discusses how broad and elusive this topic can be. Fourth, he shares several different instructor roles that he assumed in order to get students to appreciate the importance of a course in diversity.

Yellow Bird, M. J. (in press). Critical values and First Nations peoples. In R. Fong & S. Furuto (Eds.), *Culturally competent social work practice: Practice skills, interventions, and evaluation.* White Plains, NY: Longman Press.

Yuki, T. (1986). Cultural responsiveness and social work practice: An Indian clinic's success. *Health and Social Work, 11*(3), 223-229.

> This is a look at a program in a Boston hospital for American Indians. Respect for traditions and beliefs increases the relevance of the program to the population being served.

Zimmerman, M. A., Ramirez-Valles, J., Wishienki, K. M., Walter, B., & Dyer, S. (1996). The development of a measure of enculturation for Native American youth. *American Journal of Community Psychology, 24*(2), 295-310.

> This is a discussion of acculturation and enculturation based on a study of 120 American Indian youth. The article may be useful to those who wish to develop instruments or assessment tools for evaluating degree of enculturation in this or other populations.

DEAF/HARD OF HEARING

Author's note: this has been included as a separate topic since the culturally deaf do not consider themselves disabled.

Eldredge, N. M. (1993). Culturally affirmative counseling with American Indians who are deaf. *Journal of the American Deafness and Rehabilitation Association, 26*(4), 1-18.

> Deaf native children have fewer opportunities than deaf white or hearing children to learn about their identities. Residential schools for the deaf or mainstream programs for the deaf in white schools may not offer appropriate opportunities for these children to develop their identities as members of nations and tribes. This is a discussion of cultural characteristics and the interplay of identities and influences—deaf, Indian, Anglo, hearing—which affect individual clients. It includes case summaries and practice suggestions for creating a culturally affirmative environment. Suggestions include acknowledgment of tensions which exist as a result of cultural differences, incorporation of the assessment of the client's degree of acculturation into the general evaluation, and practical "tips" to develop and enhance the helping relationship. The bibliography is very helpful to those who wish to explore this topic further.

Friedlander, R. (1993). BHSM comes to the Flathead Indian reservation. *ASHA, 35*(5), 28-30.

> This is a description of efforts to provide speech, language, and hearing services on a Montana reservation. Families and children often have to travel long distances to services off reservations; as a result, accessibility to these essential services is limited. The authors stress the importance of nearby programs that are linked to on-reservation services.

Hammond, S. A., & Meineri, L. H. (1993). American Indian deaf children and youth. In K. M. Christensen & G. L. Delgado (Eds.), *Multicultural issues in deafness* (pp. 143-166). White Plains, NY: Longman Press.

> This book provides useful information and demographics, but is out of print.

Holland, S. L., Lee, B., & Lee, J. (1983). Networking services to deaf individuals on the Navajo reservation. In W. P. McCrone, R. I. Beach, & F. R. Zieziula (Eds.), *Networking and deafness: Proceedings of the national conference* (pp. 118-126). Silver Spring, MD: American Deafness and Rehabilitation Association.

McShane, D. (1980). A review of scores of American Indian children on the Wechsler Intelligence Scale. *White Cloud Journal of American Indian Health, 1*(4), 3-10.

> **The author suggests that hearing impairment as well as cultural factors can affect scores. This needs to be taken into account when interpreting results of tests such as the WIS.**

Stewart, J. L. (1992). Native American populations. *ASHA, 34*(4), 40-42.

> **The writer provides information about otitis media and communication disorders at three sites.**

Tomkins, W. (1969). *Indian Sign Language.* New York: Dover Publications.

> **First published as *Universal Indian Sign Language of the Plains Indians of North America*. This little tome may be of cultural interest to deaf/hard of hearing American Indians or others who use or are learning American Sign Language. It may also be of value in demonstrating the relationship between native and Deaf culture to American Indian students and clients. Native peoples had at one time a relatively universal sign language that appears to have been understood across the North American continent.**

Wuest, J. (1991). Harmonizing: A North American Indian approach to management of middle ear disease with transcultural nursing implications. *Journal of Transcultural Nursing, 3*(1), 5-14.

> **Middle ear disease appears to be more frequent among Indian people and is a major cause of deafness. The author discusses cultural factors which impact the management of middle ear disease by physicians and allied health professionals.**

DISABILITY, INCLUDING SPECIAL EDUCATION

Clay, J. A. (1992). Native American Independent Living. *Rural Special Education Quarterly, 11*(1), 41-50.

Conners, J., & Donnellan, A. (1993). Citizenship and culture: The role of disabled people in Navajo society. *Disability, Handicap and Society, 8*(3), 265-280.

Culture and disability [VHS]. (1988). (Available from the Native American Research and Training Center, Tucson, AZ)

> **Navajo speakers discuss the fact that the definition of disability varies across cultures, as does the response by the individual and the society. Presented at Native American Long Term Care Workshop.**

Fowler, L., Dwyer, K., Bureckmann, S., Seekins, T., Clay, J., & Locust, C. (1996). *American Indian approaches to disability policy—establishing legal protections for tribal members with disabilities: Five case studies.* Missoula, MT: Research and Training Center on Rural Rehabilitation, Montana Affiliated Rural Institute on Disabilities, University of Montana.

> **Tribes were not included under the jurisdiction of ADA and are seeking means to address this, including establishing tribal mandates and committees.**

Goodluck, C. (1991). *Use of genograms and eco-maps to assess American Indian families who have a member with a disability: Making Visible the Invisible.* (Final report: Project number R-18, pp. 1-97). Flagstaff, AZ: American Indian Rehabilitation Research and Training Center. Institute for Human Development. Northern Arizona University. (ERIC Document Reproduction Service No. ED 345 480)

Harris, G. A. (1985). Considerations in assessing English language performance of Native American children. *Topics in Language Disorders, 5*(4), 42-52.

> **This article identifies testing biases and strategies to understand speech and language use within a cultural context.**

Hodge, F., & Edmonds, R. (1988). *Socio-cultural aspects of disability: A three-area survey of disabled American Indians.* Tucson, AZ: University of Arizona Native American Research and Training Center.

Joe, J., & Miller, D. (1987). *American Indian cultural perspectives on disability.* Tucson, AZ: University of Arizona, Native American Research and Training Center.

Johnson, M. J. (1991). *American Indians and Alaska Natives with disabilities.* Washington, DC: Department of Education (Available from ERIC Document Reproduction Services No. ED 343 770).

Kazimour, K. K., & Reschly, D. J. (1981). Investigation of the norms and concurrent validity for the Adaptive Behavioral Inventory for Children (ABIC). *American Journal of Mental Deficiency, 85*(5), 512-520.

> **The article includes a summary of information about Papago youth as well as a discussion of testing bias.**

Larsson, D. G., & Larsson, E. V. (1983). Manipulating peer presence to program the generalization of verbal compliance from one-to-one in group instruction. *Education and Treatment of Children, 6*(2), 29-30.

> **This is an account of work with an selectively mute and mildly developmentally delayed American Indian student.**

Locust, C., & Lang, J. (1992). Walking in two worlds: Native Americans and the system. *American Rehabilitation, 22*(2), 2-11.

> **The authors describe an outreach program for Vocational Rehabilitation counselors working with native populations.**

Marshall, C. A. (1992). The rehabilitation needs of American Indians with disabilities in an urban setting. *Journal of Applied Rehabilitation Counseling, 22*(2), 13-21.

Marshall, C. A. (1993). The power of inquiry as regards American Indians with disabilities: Diverse manipulation or clinical necessity? *Journal of Applied Rehabilitation Counseling, 23*(4), 46-62.

Marshall, C. A., Longie, B. J., Miller, J. F., Cerveny, L. K., & Monongye, D. (1994). *A national survey of Indian health service employees and the development of a model job training demonstration project: Identifying work opportunities for American Indians and Alaska Natives with disabilities* [Executive summary]. Flagstaff, AZ: American Indian Rehabilitation Research and Training Center, Institute for Human Development (Available from Northern Arizona University, Box 5630, Flagstaff, Arizona, 86011).

McCallion, P., Janicki, M., & Grant, G.L. (1997). Exploring the impact of acculturation on older families' care giving for persons with developmental disabilities. *Family Relations, 46*(4), 347-357.

The authors include American Indian communities in their discussion and explore cultural issues which include perceptions of disability, definition of family, and expectations of family members.

Mecham, M. J. (1978). Performance of certain minority children on the Utah Test of Language Development. *Language, Speech and Hearing Services in the Schools, 9*(2), 98-102.

Miller, D. L., & Joe, J. R. (1993). Employment barriers and work rehabilitation for Navajo rehabilitation clients. *International Journal of Rehabilitation Research, 16*(2), 107-117.

The authors offer suggestions for vocational rehabilitation counselors working with native clients.

National Institute of Disability and Rehabilitation Research. (1991). *Indigenous Americans and rehabilitation, 13*(8). Washington, DC: Author

Orlansky, M. D., & Trapp, J. J. (1987). Working with Native American persons: Issues in facilitating communication and providing culturally relevant services. *Journal of Visual Impairment and Blindness, 81*(4), 151-155.

The authors give suggestions for working with American Indian students and clients with disabilities.

Orr, A. L. (1993). Training outreach workers to serve American Indian elders with visual impairment and diabetes. *Journal of Visual Impairment and Blindness, 87*(9), 336-340.

This article focuses on teaching independent living skills to clients.

Powers, L. E. (1989). Arizona RSA interactions with Native American populations. *American Rehabilitation, 15* (5/6), 32.

This is an historical review of rehabilitation services for disabled American Indians in Arizona.

Ramasamy, R. (1996). Post-high school employment: A follow-up of Apache Native American youth. *Journal of Learning Disabilities, 29*(2), 174-179.

Native youth say their lives would improve with better employment. Cultural implications are offered for the employment and transition mandates of IDEA.

Ramirez, B., & Smith, B. J. (1978). Federal mandates for the handicapped: Implications for American Indian children. *Exceptional Children, 44*(7), 521-528.

This is an history of American Indian education for the disabled and includes a discussion of the impact of federal laws and policies on disabled indigenous children.

Reschly, D. J. (1981). Evaluation of the effects of SOMPA measures classification of students as mildly mentally retarded. *American Journal of Mental Deficiency, 86*(1), 16-20.

This article contains findings on 122 Papago students. The author discusses cultural bias in testing.

Rural Special Education Quarterly [Special issues], *5*(1-4). 1984/85.

Articles from a national conference on partnership between schools and the private sector in rural America. Contains information on rural American Indian populations and training for American Indian human services workers.

Scruggs, T. E., & Cohen, S. J. (1983). A university-based summer program for a highly able but poorly achieving Indian child. *Gifted Child Quarterly, 27*(2), 90-93.

This is a single case study of an eight-year-old boy who was clearly quite intelligent, but who had poor academic performance. When academic skill deficits were remedied, the boy made significant progress. The authors provide suggestions for working with native children with poor prior academic preparation.

Stephens, N. E., & Averitt, E. L. (1993). Cultural diversity in action. *Journal of Visual Impairment and Blindness, 87*(6), 188-190.

The author discusses how Arizona Schools for the deaf and blind address needs of multicultural students.

Teeter, A. (1982). WISC-R verbal and performance abilities of Native American students referred for school learning problems. *Psychology in the Schools, 19*(1), 39-44.

Thousand, J., Rosenberg, R., Bishop, D., & Villa, R. (1997). The evolution of secondary inclusion. *Remedial and Special Education, 18*(5), 270-284.

The authors discuss ways to use native culture to develop high schools that are inclusive of adolescents with learning differences.

Toubbeh, J. I. (1985). Handicapping and disabling conditions in Native American populations. *American Rehabilitation, 11*(1), 3-8, 30-32.

U. S. Government Printing Office. (1989). *The education of students with disabilities: Where do we stand? A report to the President and Congress of the United States, 1989.* Washington, DC: Author.

This is a year-long study of students with disabilities which contains recommendations and findings.

Westby, C., & Roman, R. (1995). Finding the balance: Learning to live in two worlds. *Topics in Language Disorders, 15*(4), 68-88.

The authors believe that teaching American Indian children to understand and use narrative discourse helps them to function better in both Anglo and native culture.

DOMESTIC VIOLENCE

All Our Business [16mm color film]. (1985). (Available from Seneca Productions, Ottawa, Canada)

In this film, a wife stays with neighbors until her husband seeks help.

Arbuckle, J., Olson, L., Howard, M., Brillman, J., Anctil, C., & Sklar, D. (1996). Safe at home: Domestic violence and other homicides among women in New Mexico. *Annals of Emergency Medicine, 27*(2), 210-215.

American Indian women are at high risk for homicide as a result of domestic violence. The authors offer suggestions for decreasing this risk.

Bachman, R. (1992). *Death and violence on the reservation: Homicide, family violence, and suicide in American Indian populations.* New York: Auburn House.

Chester, B., Robin, R. W., Koss, M. P., Lopez, J., & Goldman, D. (1994). Grandmother dishonored: Violence against women by male partners in American Indian communities. *Violence and Victims, 9*(3), 249-258.

Fairchild, D. G., Fairchild, M. W., & Stoner, S. (1998). Prevalence of adult domestic violence among women seeking routine care in a Native American health care facility. *American Journal of Public Health, 88*(10), 1515-1517.

French, L. A., & Hornbuckle, J. (1979). Indian stress and violence: A psycho-cultural perspective. *Journal of Alcohol and Drug Education, 25*(2), 36-43.

Norton, I., & Manson, S. (1995). A silent minority: Battered American Indian women. *Journal of Family Violence, 10*(3), 307-318.

Profiles of 16 American Indian women seeking help with a domestic violence situation at an urban Indian health center. This article includes a mental health needs survey of 198 American Indian women.

Norton, I., & Manson, S. (1997). Domestic violence intervention in an urban Indian health center. *Community Mental Health Journal, 33*(4), 331-337.

This is a description of a successful domestic violence program which included home visits and utilized a group modality which incorporated traditional values.

Robin, R. W., Chester, B., & Rasmussen, J. K. (1998). Intimate violence in a southwestern American Indian tribal community. *Cultural Diversity and Mental Health, 4*(4), 335-344.

In this sample of 582 males and females, both genders had high exposure to domestic violence, but women were more likely to be injured. Forcible sexual assault was associated with chronic psychiatric disorders.

EDUCATION: PRIMARY AND SECONDARY

Author's note: Many of the citations in this section were graciously provided by Dr. Michael Jacobsen and Dr. Hilary Weaver from their earlier unpublished bibliography on social work and the American Indian.

Brescia, W. (1991). *Funding and resources for American Indian and Alaska Native education.* Washington, DC: Department of Education. (Available from ERIC Document Reproduction Services No. ED 348 195)

Brown, E. F., & Shaughnessy, T. (1981). *Education for social work practice with American Indian families.* Washington, DC: Department of Health and Human Services, Office of Human Development, Administration for Children, Youth and Families.

Butterfield, R. (1983). *A monograph for effectively using and developing culturally appropriate curriculum for American Indian students.* Portland, OR: Northwest Regional Educational Library.

Butterfield, R., & Pepper, F. (1991). *Improving parental participation in elementary and secondary education for American Indian and Alaska Native students.* Washington, DC: Department of Education. (Available from ERIC Document Reproduction Service No. ED 343 763)

Christensen, R. (1991). A personal perspective on tribal Alaska Native gifted and talented education. *Journal of American Indian Education, 31*, 10-14.

Daniels, R. (1988). American Indians: Gifted, talented, creative, or forgotten? *Roeper Review, 10*(4), 241-244.

Foerster, L. M. (1974). Open education and Native American values. *Educational Leadership, 32*(1), 41-45.

> Author contends that open classrooms are compatible with traditional Native American values and ways of life.

Foerster, L. M. (1977). Trends in early childhood education for Native American pupils. *Educational Leadership, 34*(5), 373-378.

Hartley, E. (1991). Through Navajo eyes: Examining differences in giftedness. *Journal of American Indian Education, 31*(1), 53-64.

Kirchenbaum, R. (1988). Methods for identifying the gifted and talented American Indian student. *Journal for the Education of the Gifted, 11*(3), 53-63.

Kopvillem, P., & Howse, J. (1992). The end of the silence. *Maclean's, 105*(37), 14-16.

LaBatte, J. (1991). Nurturing creative/artistic giftedness in American Indian students. *Journal of American Indian Education, 31*(1), 28-32.

Moore, A. J. (1987). Native Indian students and their learning styles: Research results and classroom applications. *B. C. Journal of Special Education, 11*(1), 23-37.

> The author discusses American Indian students' learning styles and teaching strategies to work with this population.

Nelson, S. R. (1982). *A study of culturally-appropriate instructional resources in Native American education: A depiction of the regional needs and resources in the Pacific Northwest.* Washington, DC: National Institute of Education. (Available from ERIC Document Reproduction Service No. ED 234 938).

Phillips, S. U. (1983). *The invisible culture: Communication in classroom and community on the Warm Springs Indian Reservation.* New York: Longman.

Rayhner, J. (1991). *Plans for dropout prevention and special school support services for American Indian and Alaska Native students.* Washington, DC: Department of Education. (ERIC Document Reproduction Service No. ED 343762).

Sanders, D. (1987). Cultural conflicts: An important factor in the academic failing of American Indian students. *Journal of Multicultural Counseling and Development, 15*(2), 81-90.

Shutiva, C. (1991). Creativity differences between reservation and urban American Indians. *Journal of American Indian Education, 31*(1), 33-52.

Swisher, K., & Deyhle, D. (1987). Styles of learning and learning of styles: Educational conflicts for American Indian/Alaska Native youth. *Journal of Multilingual and Multicultural Development, 8*(4), 345-360.

Tonemah, S. (1987). Assessing American Indian gifted and talented students' abilities. *Journal for the Education of the Gifted, 10*(3), 181-194.

Wyatt, J. D. (1978-1979). The Native teacher as culture broker. *Interchange, 9*(1), 17-27.

EDUCATION: PROFESSIONAL AND UNIVERSITY

Bending, R. L. (1997). Training child welfare workers to meet the requirements of the Indian Child Welfare Act. *Journal of Multicultural Social Work, 5*(3/4), 151-164.

Brown, E., & Shaughnessy, T. (n.d.). *Education for social work practice with American Indian families* [Training Manual]. Tempe, AZ: Arizona State University, School of Social Work.

> **This is a multivolume training manual with an instructor's guide that suggests activities for social work students or non-native practitioners who are working with American Indian clients. The manual contains activities, readings, and role plays. A comprehensive curriculum is presented, covering family customs, tribes, social networks, practice concepts with families, information on federal-tribe relationships, information on BIA, IHS, and resources. EDRS lists this as available on microfiche, paper.**

Compton, J. H. (1976). *Social work education for American Indians.* Denver, CO: University of Denver, Graduate School of Social Work.

Demarest, D. J., & Sokoloff, J. (1994). Tribal education: Reflections from the Pine Ridge Indian reservation. *Journal of Cultural Diversity, 1*(4), 70-73.

> **This article details the authors' experiences recruiting and retaining American Indian nursing students. This may be applicable to social work students.**

Edwards, D. (1984). Modeling: An important ingredient in higher education for American Indian Women Students. *Journal of the National Association of Women Deans, Administrators and Counselors, 48*(1), 31-35.

> **The author contends that role models are important in the recruitment and retention of American Indian women in colleges and universities.**

Kelly, M. L., & Nelson, C. H. (1986) A nontraditional education model with Indian indigenous social service workers. *Canadian Journal of Native Education, 13*(3), 42-55.

> **The authors discuss ways to support native social workers and appropriate roles for First Nations workers within their own cultures.** (*Author's note: Indigenous human and social service workers are often employed within the communities within which they grew up. This is a different situation than that experienced by most social workers who are based in agencies outside their communities of origin. There are unique stresses, transference, and counter-transference issues for those working in reservation settings.*)

LaFromboise, T. D., Trimble, J. E., & Mohatt, G. V. (1990). Counseling intervention and American Indian tradition: An integrative approach. *The Counseling Psychologist, 18*(4), 628-654.

Mawhiney, A., & Alcoze, T. (1989). Social work program in native human services established at Laurentian University, Sudbury, Ontario, Canada: Community alternatives. *International Journal of Family Care, 1*(2), 87-88.

Moore, A. J. (1987). Native Indian students and their learning styles: Research results and classroom applications. *B. C. Journal of Special Education, 11*(1), 23-37.

> **The author discusses American Indian students' learning styles and offers teaching strategies to work with this population.**

Pavel, D. M. (1992). *American Indian and Alaska Natives in higher education: Research on participation and graduation.* Washington, DC: National Institute of Education (Available from ERIC Document Reproduction Service No. ED 348 197)

Plumbo, M. A. (1995). Living in two different worlds or living in the world differently. *Journal of Holistic Nursing, 13*(2), 155-173.

> **American Indian nurses contribute unique qualities drawn from their traditional heritage. This article is about these nurses, but can be extended and applied to native social workers as well.**

Schiele, J. H., & Francis, E. A. (1996). The status of former CSWE ethnic minority doctoral fellows in social work education. *Journal of Social Work Education, 32*, 31-44.

Smith, A. F., & Pace, J. M. (1988). The Micmac bachelor of social work program: Policy direction and development. *Canadian Journal of Native Studies, 8*(1), 147-154.

> **This is a description of what is regarded by many as an outstanding program using offsite courses, admission of adult students, and culturally relevant pedagogy. This article may be helpful in designing a flexible program to attract minority students living on or near reservations.**

Summers, H., & Yellow Bird, M. J. (1995). Building relationships with urban First Nations community agencies: Implications for field education and research. In G. Rogers (Ed.), *Social work field education: Views and visions* (pp. 452-466). Dubuque: IA: Kendall/Hunt.

> **Building relationships with First Nations is a relatively new pursuit for schools of social work. The social work profession has had a dismal history of helping First Nations peoples achieve self-determination and actualization. This article has three objectives: to describe the experiences of the School of Social Work and the Field Education Program at the University of British Columbia (UBC) in building relationships with First Nations communities and agencies; to describe the experiences of the UBC School of Social Work in developing practica sites in First Nations agencies; and to describe the innovative and creative teaching and practice principles that are used by various First Nations agencies to educate social work practica students.**

Tate, D. S., & Schwartz, C. L. (1993). Increasing the retention of American Indian students in professional programs in higher education. *Journal of American Indian Education, 33*(1), 21-31.

> **American Indians have a high rate of dropout from higher education programs, including social work. This survey of 84 social work students identifies factors contributing to their leaving higher education and includes suggestions to improve retention.**

Weaver, H. N. (1999). Transcultural nursing with Native Americans: Critical knowledge, skills, and attitudes. *Journal of Transcultural Nursing, 10*(3), 197-202.

> **This article focuses on nursing, but has implications for social work.**

Weaver, H. N. (in press). Indigenous nurses and professional education: Friends or foes? *Journal of Nursing Education.*

Weaver, H. N. (in press). The professional training of Native American psychologists: A comfortable fit or more cultural loss? *Transformations.*

White, J. (1994). Has social work education failed the First Nations? *Proceedings of the First Annual Conference of First Nations Social Work Educators.* Lawrence, KS: University of Kansas, School of Social Welfare.

> **The author looks at the history and statistical data on First Nations social work faculty and graduate students and concludes that this population has been underrepresented in social work education and tends to be hired at lower ranks and in non-tenure track positions. The author also explores reasons why First Nations students are not attracted to social work programs and why there is a high rate of drop-out.**

Yellow Bird, M. (1998). *Invited commentary on multicultural social work education—A perspective on community practice.* Conference for Culturally Competent Social Work Education in the 21st Century. Ann Arbor, MI.

> **Understanding and implementing multiculturalism and cultural competency frameworks in community social work practice curriculums are critical to social justice. This paper reviews Felix Rivera's perspectives on community practice and finds considerable agreement with his ideas.**

Yellow Bird, M. (1999). Radical, skewed, benign, and calculated: Reflections on teaching diversity. *Reflections, Narratives of Professional Helping: A Journal for the Helping Professions, 4*(2), 13-22.

> This article is a narrative that shares the author's experience teaching diversity in an undergraduate social work program. First, he shares experiences teaching diversity as a Ph.D. student. Second, he discusses how teaching social work with First Nations in Canada influenced his later teaching of diversity. Third, he attempts to define diversity and discusses how broad and elusive this topic can be. Fourth, he shares several different instructor roles that he assumed in order to get students to appreciate the importance of a course in diversity.

EMPOWERMENT

Yellow Bird, M. (1999). Indian, American Indian, and Native Americans: Counterfeit identities. *Winds of Change: A Magazine for American Indian Education and Opportunity, 14*(1), 86.

> In this critical essay, the author argues that Indian, American Indian, and Native American are inaccurate, confusing, and colonized identities. He maintains that the continued use of these terms is oppressive and that the scholarship about First Nations peoples must be decolonized through the use of more empowering descriptors.

Yellow Bird, M. J., & Chenault, V. (1999). The role of social work in advancing indigenous education: Obstacles and promises in empowerment-oriented social work practice. In K. Swisher & J. Tippeconnic (Eds.), *Next steps: Research and practice to advance Indian education* (pp. 201-235). (ERIC Document Reproduction Service No. ED 427 911).

> The professional mission of social work and the roles of social workers can advance the practice of indigenous peoples' education. Empowerment-oriented social work practices illustrate how this is possible. To create change, educators and social workers must develop strong collaborative relationships with social workers. This article examines several ways educators and social workers can use empowerment-oriented social work practice to improve the education of First Nations students. First, it examines historical and structural obstacles to advancing indigenous peoples' education. Second, it discusses how the professional behavior, education, and roles of social workers can help address several micro and macro issues preventing the advancement of First Nations education.

FAMILIES

Bowman, B. J. (1997). Cultural pathways towards Antonovsky's Sense of Coherence. *Journal of Clinical Psychology, 53*(2), 139-142.

> The author suggests that native families may have a moral and religious orientation, in contrast to Anglo families who may value achievement and independence more highly.

Brown, E. F., & Shaughnessy, T. (1981). *Education for social work practice with American Indian families* [Manual]. Washington, DC: Department of Health and Human Services, Office of Human Development, Administration for Children, Youth and Families.

This manual has relevant information on understanding and working with American Indian families.

Canda, E. R., & Yellow Bird, M. J. (1997). Another view, cultural strengths are crucial. *Families in Society: The Journal of Contemporary Human Services, 78*(3), 248.

The entire community is the most effective clinic. This article provides a short commentary of how cultural strengths are crucial in the development of culturally competent strategies for AOD abuse treatment.

Dene Family [VHS]. (n.d). (Available from Dr. Otto Schaefer Resource Center, Department of Health, Government of the Northwest Territories, Yellowknife, Canada)

This film depicts the daily life of a Dene family in an isolated rural village.

Embree, B. G., & DeWitt, M. L. (1997). Family background characteristics and relationship satisfaction in a native community in Canada. *Social Biology, 44*(102), 42-54.

The author explores factors during growing-up years that affect later marital and partner satisfaction. The impact of child sexual abuse and its correlation with alcohol consumption is also discussed. Parent role modeling is identified as important to adjustment to adult role and responsibilities.

Gilliard, F. D., Mahler, R., & Davis, S. M. (1998). Health-related quality of life for rural American Indians in New Mexico. *Ethnicity and Health, 3*(3), 223-229.

This telephone survey of over 600 American Indians is considered by the authors to be an efficient tool for data collection with this population. Over half reported their health to be representative of that of the rural American Indian population reported in the 1990 census. See Pearson et al., for another perspective on the use of the telephone for data collection in this population. (cf: Research)

Goodluck, C. (1980). Strength of caring. *Social Casework, 61*(8), 519-521.

This is a discussion of child care customs and the role of extended family. The author provides case examples, along with a call for recognition of strengths of Indian peoples.

Goodluck, C. (1980). Working with American Indian parents: A cultural approach. *Social Casework, 61*(8), 471-475.

Goodluck, C., & Bane, W. (1984). *Informal helping: Making it work for children, youth and families.* Denver, CO: University of Denver, Family Resource Center.

Harachi, W. W., Catalano, R. F., & Hawkins, J. D. (1997). Effective recruitment for parenting programs within ethnic minority communities. *Child and Adolescent Social Work Journal, 14*(1), 23-39.

Herring, R. D. (1989). The American native family: Dissolution by coercion. *Journal of Multicultural Counseling and Development, 17*(1), 4-13.

Jacobs, C., & Bowles, D. D. (1988). Cultural evolution of American Indian families. In *Ethnicity and race: Critical concepts in social work*. Silver Spring, MD: NASW.

Johnson, C. A., & Johnson, D. L. (1998). Working with Native American families. *New Directions for Mental Health Services, 77*(2), 89-96.

Lewis, R. G. (1980). *Strengths of the American Indian family* [Resource paper for the National Indian Child Abuse and Neglect Resource Center]. Tulsa, OK: National Indian Child Abuse and Neglect Resource Center.

Light, H. K. (1986). American Indian families. *Journal of American Indian Education, 26*(1), 1-5.

Metcalf, A. (1978). *A model for treatment in a Native American family service center*. Oakland, CA: Urban Indian Child Resource Center.

Nybell, L. M. (1984). *Serving American Indian families and children: A sourcebook in child welfare*. Ann Arbor, MI: National Child Welfare Training Center, School of Social Work, University of Michigan.

Red Horse, J., Lewis, R., Feit, M., & Decker, J. (1978). Family behavior of urban American Indians. *Social Casework, 59*(2), 67-72.

Red Horse, J. G. (1980). American Indian elders: Unifiers of Indian families. *Social Casework, 61*(8), 490-493.

> **The author discusses the role of the elder in the American Indian family, and ways in which human services workers can utilize elders.** *(Author's note: The term "elder" within a native context does not necessarily refer to age, but is bestowed upon those viewed as possessing wisdom and providing leadership to the family, clan, or tribe.)*

Red Horse, J. G. (1980). Family structure and value orientation in American Indians. *Social Casework, 61*(8), 462-467.

> **This paper discusses not only family structures, but also developmental phases of American Indian families.**

Robinson, Z. (1996). Serving Native American children and families: Considering cultural variables. *Language, Speech and Hearing Services in Schools, 27*(4), 373-384.

Swenson, J., & Rosenthail, G. (Eds.). (1980). *Warm Springs: A case study approach to recognizing the strengths of American Indian and Alaska Native families*. Washington, DC: American Academy of Child Psychiatry.

Unger, S. (Ed.). (1977). *The destruction of American Indian families*. New York: Association of American Indian Affairs.

> **This is a collection of papers on the child welfare crisis and the status of American Indian families. It includes testimony presented to the Senate Subcommittee on Indian Affairs.**

Weaver, H., & White, B. J. (1997). The Native American family circle: Roots of resiliency. *Journal of Family Social Work, 2*(1), 67-79.

> This article describes American Indian families and the history and context within which social workers must practice, as well as techniques for intervention.

Yellow Bird, M., & Snipp, M. C. (1994). American Indian families. In R. C. Taylor (Ed.), *Minority families in the United States: A multicultural perspective* (pp. 170-201). New York: Prentice-Hall.

> The body of work on First Nations families is relatively small when compared to the amount of research on other racial ethnic groups in the United States. This article first reviews available demographic data with respect to household composition, marriage and divorce, family structure and economic well-being, labor force participation, education, and patterns of intermarriage. Second, the literature on First Nations families is examined with special attention to cultural lifestyle, role status, authority, and family values and socialization.

FETAL ALCOHOL SYNDROME (FAS)

Author's note: Because of its prevalence in American Indian communities, FAS is given a separate section from health.

Abel, E. L. (1995). An update on incidence of FAS: FAS is not an equal opportunity birth defect. *Neurotoxicology and Teratology, 17*(2), 437-443.

> American Indian rates of fetal alcohol syndrome are ten times greater than among Caucasians. However, the authors suggest that FAS may be more correlated with low socio-economic status than with racial or ethnic status.

Alcohol and the unborn baby [Slide presentation, 45 slides]. (n. d.). (Available from White Mountain Apache Tribe, White River, AZ)

> This is a slide presentation demonstrating effects of drinking and using drugs during pregnancy. The goal is to encourage abstinence.

Broken cord [VHS]. (1992). (Available from PBS Video, Alexandria, VA)

> Authors Louise Erdrich and Michael Dorris discuss effects of FAS on their adopted son and on American Indian nations.

Masis, K. B., & May, P. A. (1991). A comprehensive local program for the prevention of fetal alcohol syndrome. *Public Health Reports, 106*(5), 484-489.

May, P. A., & Hymbaugh, K. J. (1989). A macro-level fetal alcohol syndrome prevention program for Native Americans and Alaska Natives: Description and evaluation. *Journal of Studies on Alcohol, 50*(6), 508-518.

HEALTH

American Indian Health Care Association. (1992). *Native American health promotion and disease prevention bibliography* (3rd ed.). St. Paul, MN: Author.

Berry, J. W. (1985). Acculturation among circumpolar peoples: Implications for health status. *Arctic Medical Research, 40,* 21-27.

Boehnlein, J. K., Kinsei, J. D., Leung, P. K., Matsunaga, D., Johnson, R., & Shore, J. H. (1992/1993). The natural history of medical and psychiatric disorders in an American Indian community. *Culture, Medicine and Psychiatry, 16*(4), 543-554.

> **The authors explain that alcoholism and related disorders, including cardiovascular diseases and diabetes, are prevalent and need more attention in this population.**

Boyce. W. T., & Boyce, J. C. (1983). Acculturation and changes in health among Navajo boarding school students. *Social Science and Medicine, 17*(4), 219-226.

Buehler, J. A. (1992). Traditional Crow Indian health beliefs and practices: Toward a grounded theory. *Journal of Holistic Nursing, 10*(1), 18-33.

> **The American Indian view of wellness is holistic. This article looks at patterns of traditional health practices and the types of traditional health practices in common use among indigenous peoples in the U.S.**

Chief Two Tree, Cherokee medicine man [VHS]. (1986). (Available from School of Medicine, East Carolina University, Greenville, NC)

Cohen, K. (1998). Native American medicine. *Alternative Therapies in Health and Medicine, 4*(6), 45-57.

> **This is a comprehensive overview of native healing in North America. The author emphasizes the importance of seeking wholeness and harmony in the native paradigms of health and healing.**

Communicating with Native American patients [VHS]. (1988). (Available from Native American Research Training Center, Tuscon, AZ)

> **A Navajo health care provider discusses communication issues, ways to establish a relationship, ways of ensuring patient compliance, the use of interpreters, and working with native healing personnel.**

Conners, J., & Donnellan, A. (1993). Citizenship and culture: The role of disabled people in Navajo society. *Journal of Rehabilitation Counseling, 22*(2), 265-280.

Cultural sensitivity in health and healing [VHS]. (1989). (Available from NAU Television Services, Flagstaff, AZ)

> **This is an address by a professor of nursing who emphasizes that cultural differences should be acknowledged by health care providers.**

Davis, S. M., Hunt, K., & Tso, H. (1990). Oral histories and traditions: An intergenerational approach to health promotion. *Journal of Navajo Education, 7*(3), 23-27.

DeMars, P. A. (1992). An occupational therapy life skills curriculum model for a Native American tribe: A health promotion program based on ethnographic field research. *American Journal of Occupational Therapy, 46*(8), 727-736.

> **Although its focus is occupational therapy, this model curriculum draws on cultural context in British Columbia to suggest ways health professionals can provide preventive services and life skills training for native populations.**

Dubray, W., & Sanders, A. (1999). Interaction between American Indian ethnicity and health care. *Journal of Health and Social Policy, 10*(4), 67-84.

Gilliard, F. D., Mahler, R., & Davis, S. M. (1998). Health-related quality of life for rural American Indians in New Mexico. *Ethnicity and Health, 3*(3), 223-229.

> **This telephone survey of over 600 American Indians is considered by the authors to be an efficient tool for data collection with this population. Over half reported their health to be representative of that of the rural American Indian population reported in the 1990 census. See Pearson et al., for another perspective on the use of the telephone for data collection in this population. (cf: Research)**

Good medicine [VHS]. (1980). (Available from WQED, Pittsburgh, PA)

> **This is a PBS documentary on native views of health. It shows healing rituals and looks at what indigenous nations can offer traditional western medicine.**

Grossman, D. C., Sugarman, J. R., Fox, C., & Moran, J. (1997). Motor-vehicle crash-injury risk factors among American Indians. *Accident Analysis and Prevention, 29*(3), 313-319.

> **American Indian and Alaska Natives have the highest rates of mortality due to motor vehicle accidents of any ethnic group. The authors state that alcohol impairment and failure in this population to use seat belts appear to be significant factors, especially in rural areas.**

Hammerschlag, C. A. (1988). *The dancing healers: A doctor's journey of healing with Native Americans.* San Francisco: Harper & Row.

Hurlinger, K. W., & Tanner, D. (1994). The peyote way: Implications for culture care theory. *Journal of Transcultural Nursing, 5*(2), 5-11.

> **The authors present a traditional healing of a Navajo man who has experienced a stroke, including a description of a Native peyote ceremony, in order to stress the benefits of traditional healing methods.**

Johnson, M. J. (1991). *American Indians and Alaska Natives with disabilities.* Washington, DC: Department of Education. (Available from ERIC Document Reproduction Service No. ED 343 770)

Kim, C., & Kwow, Y. S. (1998). Navajo use of native healers. *Archives of Internal Medicine, 158*(20), 2245-2249.

> **Over two-thirds of Navajo patients use native healers, according to the authors, although many also use a combination of Western and traditional medicine.**

Krippner, K. (1995). A cross-cultural comparison of four healing models. *Alternative Therapies in Health and Medicine, 1*(1), 21-29.

> The majority of people in the world use nonwestern medical treatments. The authors provide a 12-point model for the understanding of alternative medical systems.

Kunitz, S. (1983). *Disease change and the role of medicine: The Navajo experience.* Berkeley, CA: University of California Press.

> This is a discussion of the role of modern medical techniques within traditional Navajo healing practices.

LaMarine, R. J. (1987). Self-esteem, health locus of control and health attitudes among Native American children. *Journal of School Health, 57*(9), 371-374.

Lewis, T. H. (1990). *The medicine men: Oglala Sioux ceremony and healing.* Lincoln, NE: University of Nebraska Press.

Lightdale, J. R., Oken, E., Klein, W. M., Landrigan, P. J., & Welty, T. K. (1997). Psychosocial barriers to health promotion in an American Indian population. *American Indian and Alaska Native Mental Health Research, 7*(3), 34-49.

> The authors contend that beliefs about health and health risks may prevent successful medical intervention. This study is based on a sample of 200 individuals.

Locust, C. (1985). *American Indian beliefs concerning health and unwellness.* Tucson, AZ: University of Arizona, Native American Research and Training Center.

Manson, S. P., & Dinges, N. G. (Eds.). (1988). Behavioral health issues among American Indians and Alaska Natives: Explorations on the frontiers of the biobehavioral sciences. *American Indian and Alaska Native Mental Health Research Monograph Series, 1*(1). (ERIC Document Reproduction Service No. ED 326 336).

Many Deeds, M. (1992). The reason why smoking is non-traditional. *American Indian Community House Community Bulletin,* Winter, 14.

Marbella, A. M., Harris, M. C., Diehr, S., & Ignace, G. (1998). Use of Native American healers among Native American patients in an urban American health center. *Archives of Family Medicine, 7*(2), 182-185.

> American Indians may use alternative forms of treatment and often value their healer's advice. The authors warn that care providers need to be aware of this and respectful toward these attitudes.

Marshall, C. A. (1992). The rehabilitation needs of American Indians with disabilities in an urban setting. *Journal of Applied Rehabilitation Counseling, 22*(2), 13-21.

McClure, L., & Boulanger, M. (1993). *First Nations urban health bibliography: A review of the literature and exploration of strategies* [Northern Health Unit Monograph Series]. Manitoba, Canada: University of Manitoba.

McClure, L., Boulanger, M., Kaufer, J., & Forsyth, S. (1992). *First Nations urban health bibliography: Review of the literature and exploration of strategies.* Winnipeg, Canada: Northern Health Research Unit, University of Winnipeg.

McShane, D. (1987). Mental health and North American Indian/Native communities: Cultural transactions, education, and regulation. *American Journal of Community Psychology, 15*(1), 95-116.

Mehi-Madrona, L. E. (1999). Native American medicine in the treatment of chronic illness: Developing an integrated program and evaluating its effectiveness. *Alternative Therapies in Health and Medicine, 5*(1), 36-44.

Meketon, M. J. (1983). Indian mental health: An orientation. *American Journal of Orthopsychiatry, 53*(1), 110-115.

Michielutte, R., Sharp, P. C., Dignan, M. B., & Blinson, K. (1994). Cultural issues in the development of cancer control programs for American Indian populations. *Journal of Health Care for the Poor and Underserved, 5*(4), 280-296.

Moncher, M. S., Schinke, S.P., Holden, G., W., & Aragon, S. (1989). Tobacco use by American Indian youth. *Journal of the American Medical Association, 262*(11), 1469.

Rokala, D. A., Bruce, S. G., & Meikeljohn, C. (1991). *Diabetes mellitus in Native populations of North America: An annotated bibliography.* Winnipeg, Canada: Northern Health Research Unit, University of Manitoba.

Schinke, S. P., Gilchrist, L.D., Schilling, R. F., Walker, R.D., Locklear, V. S., & Kitajima, E. (1986). Smokeless tobacco use among Native American adolescents. *New England Journal of Medicine, 314*(16), 1051-1052.

Schinke, S. P., Schilling, R. F. II, Gilchrist, L. D., Ashby, M. R., & Kitajima, E. (1987). Pacific Northwest Native American youth and smokeless tobacco use. *The International Journal of the Addictions, 22*(9), 881-884.

Wakegijig, R., Roy, A., & Hayward, C. (1988). Traditional medicine: An Anishinabek nation perspective. *Environments, 19*(3), 122-124.

Waldram, J. B. (1990). The persistence of traditional medicine in urban areas: The case of Canada's Indians. *American Indian and Alaska Mental Health Research, 4*(1), 9-29.

Weaver, H. N. (1999). Health concerns for Native American youth: A culturally grounded approach to health promotion. *Journal of Human Behavior in the Social Environment, 2*(1/2), 127-143.

Wilson, C., Civic, D., & Glass, D. (1995). Prevalence and correlates of depressive symptoms among adults visiting an Indian Health Service primary care clinic. *American Indian and Alaska Native Mental Health Research, 6*(2), 1-12.

HEALTH: MATERNAL-CHILD

Association of Iroquois and Allied Indians. (1991). *Bonding circle of breast feeding* [VHS with a poster and brochures]. (Available from Chromavision International, Gloucester, Canada)

The film presents the advantages of breast feeding, the psychology of bonding, and the importance of introducing the baby to siblings. It is designed to encourage indigenous mothers to nurse their babies. This might be interesting to use in HBSE and courses on childhood development to show the impact of industrialization and commercial infant formula sales on the well-being of indigenous and third-world infants.

Kvigne, V. L., Bull, L. B., Welty, T. K., Leonardson, G. R., & Lacina, L. (1998). Relationship of prenatal alcohol use with maternal and prenatal factors in American Indian women. *Social Biology, 45*(3/4), 214-222.

Sugarman, J. R., Brenneman, G., LaRoque, W., Warren, C. W., & Goldberg, H. L. (1994). The urban American Indian oversample in the 1988 National Maternal and Infant Health Survey. *Public Health Reports, 109*(2), 243-250.

Two-thirds of American Indian and Alaska natives live in urban settings, and yet this article shows that there is little information about maternal-child health risk factors in this population. Poverty, difficulty and delays in obtaining prenatal care, as well as lack of health coverage were also reported as more frequent among American Indians.

Tyson, H., Higgins, R. D., & Tyson, I. (1999). Family dysfunction and Native American women who do not seek prenatal care. *Archives of Family Medicine, 8*(2), 111-117.

HIV/AIDS

A chance for change [VHS]. (1990). (Available from Gryphon Productions, Limited, Vancouver, Canada)

A First Nations man leaves prison and returns home to the reserve. His wife wants him to be tested for AIDS, and he agrees to do so. The film focuses on responsibility and lifestyle changes.

AIDS and the Native American family [Film]. (1990). (Available from Upstream Productions, Seattle, WA)

This film is about a family with AIDS, in which the wife is pregnant. The film emphasizes the importance of spirituality in prevention and intervention.

American Indians against HIV/AIDS leadership project [VHS]. (1991). (Available from the University of North Dakota, Department of Family Medicine, Grand Forks, MN)

This program is designed to educate American Indian people about HIV/AIDS.

Circle of warriors [VHS]. (1989). (Available from the National Native American AIDS Prevention Center, Oakland, CA)

Ten American Indians discuss living with HIV/AIDS. The video portrays their responses to discovering their condition, the type of help they would like to have, and the use of the medicine wheel in coping with the syndrome.

Conway, G., Ambrose, T. J., Epistein, M. R., Chase, E., Johannes, P., Hooper, E. Y., & Helgerson, S. D. (1992). Prevalence of HIV and AIDS in American Indian and Alaska Natives. *The IHS Primary Care Provider, 17*(5), 65-69.

David's song: American Indian teens and AIDS [VHS]. (1988). (Available from the University of New Mexico Center for Indian Youth Program Development, Albuquerque, NM)

> **Teens interview a native man with AIDS and discuss prevention. This may be useful as trigger for youth discussion groups.**

DePoy, E., & Bolduc, C. (1997). AIDS prevention in a rural American Indian population: A collaborative effort between community providers. In L. B. Brown (Ed.), *Two spirit people: American Indian lesbian women and gay men* (pp. 97-108). New York: Harrington Park Press.

Face to face: Native Americans living with AIDS [VHS]. (1989). (Available from the National Native American AIDS Prevention Center, Oakland, CA)

> **This is a series of interviews with persons with AIDS/HIV and their parents and relatives.**

Fighting for our lives: Women confronting AIDS [VHS]. (1990). (Available from the Center for Women's Policy Studies, Washington, DC)

> **This video presents information on AIDS and minority women, including a segment on a health education facility serving American Indians.**

I'm not afraid of me [VHS]. (1991). (Available from the Alaska Native Health Board, Anchorage, AK)

> **This is a documentary showing the lives of a woman and her daughter who have HIV/AIDS as they interact in discussion about how they contracted the disease, and its impact on their current functioning and future plans.**

It can happen to anybody [VHS]. (1990). (Available from Kahnawake Social Services, Kahnawake, Canada)

> **Two people with AIDS talk about how their community and families responded to learning about their illness.**

Native American Leadership Commission on Health and AIDS. (1994). *A Native American leadership response to HIV and AIDS.* New York: American Indian Community House.

Rowell, R. (1997). Developing AIDS services for Native Americans: Rural and urban contrasts. In L. B. Brown (Ed.), *Two spirit people: American Indian lesbian women and gay men* (pp. 85-96). New York: Harrington Park Press.

Weaver, H. N. (1999). Through indigenous eyes: A Native American perspective on the HIV epidemic. *Health and Social Work, 24*(1), 27-34.

MENTAL HEALTH

Abbott, P. J. (1998). Traditional and western healing practices for alcoholism in American Indians and Alaska Natives. *Substance Use and Misuse, 33*(13), 2605-2646.

A variety of healing practices such as sacred dances, sweat lodges, and the talking circle have been used in treatment along with such Western approaches as medication and detoxification. The author explains how Native communities have used both approaches to meet their needs. These are applicable to mental health as well as to substance abuse.

Angell, G. B. (1997). Madness in the family: The "windigo." *Journal of Family Social Work, 2*(2), 179-196.

This article examines how northeastern native peoples of the Alquonqian group use the concept of the windigo to explain why bad things happen. This concept is a means of empowerment of the person as well as a way to separate the individual from the problem.

Brendtro, L. K., & Brokenleg, M. (1993). Beyond the curriculum of control. *Journal of Emotional and Behavioral Problems, 1*(4), 5-11.

The authors discuss the use of an empowerment model within a native paradigm to treat behavior problems.

Dufrene, P. M., & Coleman, V. D. (1992). Counseling Native Americans: Guidelines for group process. *The Journal for Specialists in Group Work, 17,* 229-234.

Griffin-Pierce, T. (1997). When I am lonely, the mountains call me: The impact of sacred geography on Navajo psychological well being. *American Indian and Alaska Native Mental Health Research, 7*(3), 1-10.

The author explores emotional ties to the land and the psychological disconnection traditional peoples experience when dislocated from geographic homelands. Spirituality and land are inextricably united in traditional culture.

Grossman, D. C., Putsch, R. W., & Inui, T. (1993). The meaning of death to adolescents in an American Indian community. *Family Medicine, 25*(9), 593-597.

There is a high mortality rate among young American Indian people. The authors explore this, along with beliefs about death, sickness, healing, and Spirit Sickness.

Jilek, W. G. (1984). *Salish Indian mental health and culture change: Psychogenic and therapeutic aspects of the Guardian Spirit ceremonial.* Toronto, Canada: Holt, Rinehart and Winston.

Jilek, W. G., & Todd, N. (1974). Witch doctors succeed where doctors fail: Psychotherapy among coastal Salish Indians. *Canadian Psychiatric Association Journal, 19*(4), 351-356.

Kahn, M. W. (1986). Psychosocial disorders of aboriginal peoples of the United States and Australia. *Journal of Rural Community Psychology, 7*(1), 45-59.

Kelson, D. R., & Attneave, C. L. (1981). *Bibliography of North American Indian mental health.* Westport, CT: Greenwood.

LaFromboise, T. (1988). American Indian mental health policy. *American Psychologist, 43*(5), 388-397.

LaFromboise, T. D., Trimble, J. E., & Mohatt, G. V. (1990). Counseling intervention and American Indian tradition: An integrative approach. *The Counseling Psychologist, 18*(4), 628-654.

McShane, D. (1987). Mental health and North American Indian and Native communities: Cultural transaction, education, and regulation. *American Journal of Community Psychology, 15*(1), 95-116.

McSwain, K. (1998). *Annotated bibliography for an anthropological inquiry into First Nations mental health* [On-line]. Available: *http://www.rpnam.mb.ca/bibfile.html*

> **This is a 13-page bibliography exploring and analyzing mental health issues within First Nations, emphasizing nations within Canada and focusing in particular on women's perspectives. This site links to an associated website, Registered Psychiatric Nurses Association of Manitoba, and to various other thematic sites related to the bibliographic citations.**

Meketon, M. J. (1983). Indian mental health. *American Journal of Orthopsychiatry, 53*(1), 110-115.

Napholz, L. (1995). Mental health and American Indian women's multiple roles. *American Indian and Alaska Native Mental Health Research, 6*(2), 57-75.

> **This article examines the sex roles and psychological well-being among 148 American Indian working women.**

O'Nell, T. D. (1992/1993). Feeling worthless: An investigation of depression and problem drinking at the Flathead Reservation. *Culture, Medicine and Psychiatry, 16*(4), 447-469.

> **The author focuses on cultural factors including the disruption of social bonds and cultural demoralization that contribute to substance abuse, depression, and suicidality.**

Red Horse, Y., Gonzales-Santin, E., Beane, S., & Tolson-Gonzales, P. A. (1981). *Traditional and non-traditional community mental health services with American Indians.* Tempe, AZ: American Indian Projects for Community Development, Training and Research, Arizona State University.

Richards, E. H. (1981). Cultural and historical perspectives in counseling American Indians. In S. W. Derald (Ed.), *Counseling the culturally different: Theory and practice* (pp.102-117). New York: John Wiley & Sons.

Robin, R. W., Chester, B., Rasmussen, J. K., Jaranson, J. M., & Goldman, D. (1997). Prevalence and characteristics of trauma and post-traumatic stress disorder in a southwestern American Indian community. *American Journal of Psychiatry, 154*(11), 1582-1588.

> **American Indian subjects in this 247 person sample had a higher rate of trauma with post-traumatic stress disorder than the general U. S. population.**

Saint-Amand, N., & Clavette, H. (1992). *Self-help and mental health beyond psychiatry.* Ottawa, Canada: Canadian Council on Social Development.

Smith, M. A. (1990). Psychiatric function and roles in an Indian health program context. *American Indian and Alaska Native Mental Health Research , 4*(1), 41-52.

Thomason, T. (1991). Counseling Native Americans: An introduction for non-Native American counselors. *Journal of Counseling and Development, 69*(4), 321-327.

Timpson, J. (1984). Indian mental health: Changes in the delivery of care in Northwestern Ontario. *Canadian Psychiatric Association Journal, 29*(42), 234-241.

Timpson, J. (1988). Depression in a Native Canadian in Northwestern Ontario: Sadness, grief, or spiritual illness? *Canada's Mental Health, 36*(2/3), 5-8.

Trimble, J. E. (1987). Self perception and perceived alienation among American Indians. *Journal of Community Psychology, 15*(3), 316-333.

Walker, R. D., Lambert, M. D., Walker, P. S., & Kivlaham, D. R. (1992/1993). Treatment implications of comorbid psychopathology in American Indian and Alaska Natives. *Culture, Medicine and Psychiatry, 16*(4), 555-572.

> **The authors suggest that barriers to treatment, including lack of appropriate interventions, may interfere with American Indian populations' use of available treatment resources. The article also includes information about Western and traditional approaches to treatment.**

White Cloud Center. (1981). *Bibliography of North American Indian mental health.* Westport, CT: Greenwood.

Wilson, C., Civic, D., & Glass, D. (1995). Prevalence and correlates of depressive symptoms among adults visiting an Indian Health Service primary care clinic. *American Indian and Alaska Native Mental Health Research, 6*(2), 1-12.

PARENTING

Gonzalez-Santin, E. (n.d.) *The White Mountain child protection service training curriculum: Nohwii chaghashe baa da gontzaa (protect our Apache children)* [Training Manual]. White River, AZ: White Mountain Apache Tribe. (Available from Arizona State University, School of Social Work, Box 871802, Tempe, AZ 85287-1802).

> **This is a comprehensive training manual providing information on native communities, lifestyles, and medical and sociological issues including risk factors for abuse. Also included are legal issues in federal and tribal law, CPS procedures and protocols, tribal community practice, healing and wellness in an indigenous context, and teaching tools and tips for trainers.**

Goodluck, C., & Short, D. (1980). Working with American Indian parents: A cultural approach. *Social Casework, 61*(8), 472-475.

Horejsi, C., Craig, B. H., & Pablo, J. (1992). Reactions by Native American parents to child protection agencies: Cultural and community factors. *Child Welfare, 71*(4), 329-342.

> **The authors explain the impact of oppression on the ability of parents to accept help from child welfare agencies. They also provide a guide to understanding and working with American Indian parents.**

Seidman, R. Y., Williams, R., Burns, P., Jacobson, S., Weatherby, F., & Primeaux, M. (1994). Cultural sensitivity in assessing urban Native American parenting. *Public Health Nursing, 11*(2), 98-103.

Yellow Bird, M. (1999). Indigenous peoples' parenting. In C. A. Smith (Ed.), *Encyclopedia of parenting* (pp. 231-233). New York: Greenwood/Plenum.

> **This article focuses on indigenous peoples' diversity, identity, and parenting roles before European contact. It identifies several events that were disruptive to indigenous peoples' parent roles and suggests ten principles that may help indigenous parents promote positive parent-child relationships that do not interfere with cultural beliefs.**

POLICY, HISTORY, AND SOCIAL WELFARE

Author's note: Policy has been broadly defined to incorporate a number of approaches. Information on laws, history, economic and community development, social justice and advocacy, concepts, and social policies are among the materials included.

AIDL Survey Results. (1994/1995). *Rural facts: American Indian disability legislation project* [On-line]. Missoula, MT: University of Montana. Available: *http://ruralinstitute.umt.edu/rtcrural/ I...Factsheets/indian_legislation_survey.htm*

> **This website provides a survey of Indian tribal governments with respect to disability issues, policies, and services.**

Brave Heart, M. Y., & DeBruyn, L. M. (1998). The American Indian holocaust: Healing historical unresolved grief. *American Indian and Alaska Native Mental Health Research, 8*(2), 56-78.

> **The impact of losses resulting from European contact include unresolved grief across generations. This contributes to the high rates of social pathology among native peoples. The authors draw upon holocaust literature and suggest interventions for healing this trauma. This is a seminal article that gave rise to considerable interest in the relationship between historic unresolved grief and the current situation of indigenous peoples in the U.S. and Canada.**

Brief history of U.S. laws applied to American Indians [On-line]. Missoula, MT: University of Montana. Available: *http://ruralinstitute.umt.edu/rtcrural/Indian/Factsheets/AIDL_History.htm*

Brown, E. F. (1978). American Indians in modern society: Implications for social policy and services. In D. G. Norton (Ed.), *The dual perspective: Inclusion of ethnic minority content in the social work curriculum* (pp. 68-80). New York: Council on Social Work Education.

Brown, E. F. (1978). *A conceptual framework for the study and analysis of Indian communities.* Tempe, AZ: American Indian Projects for Community Development, Training, and Research, Arizona State University, School of Social Work.

Cassidy, F. (1991). Aboriginal self-determination. *Proceedings of a Conference Held September 30-October 3, 1990.* Winnipeg, Canada: The Institute for Research on Public Policy.

Champagne, D. (Ed.). (1994). *The Native North American almanac: A reference work on Native North Americans in the U.S. and Canada.* Detroit, MI: Gale Research.

> **This volume provides a wealth of information on history, culture, art, religion, media, economy, and contemporary status of American Indians. It includes biographies and a glossary of terms.**

Charleston, G. M., & King, J. L. (1991). *Indian nations at risk task force: Listen to the people.* Washington, DC: Department of Education. (Available from ERIC Document Reproduction Service No. ED 343 754)

Churchill, W. (Ed.). (1990). *Critical issues in Native North America* [WGIA Document 62]. Copenhagen, Denmark: The International Secretariat of International Work Group for Indigenous Affairs.

> **This is a series of essays by indigenous authors on topics relevant to native peoples. Cultural assimilation, genocide, political resistance, and seizure of lands are among the topics covered.**

Cingolani, W. (1973). Acculturating the Indian: Federal Policies, 1834-1973. *Social Work, 18,* 24-29.

> **This is an historic overview of federal Indian policies during this time period. The article discusses reasons for failure of policies.**

Dyck, N. (1993). Telling it like it is: Some dilemmas of fourth world ethnography and advocacy. In N. Dyck & J. Waldram (Eds.), *Anthropology, public policy, and native peoples in Canada.* Montreal, Canada: McGill-Queen's University Press.

Edwards, E. D., & Smith, L. L. (1979). A brief history of American Indian social policy. *Journal of the Humanities, 7*(2), 52-64.

Engelstad, D., & Bird, J. (1992). *Nation to nation: Aboriginal sovereignty and the future of Canada.* Toronto, Canada: Citizens for Public Justice.

Green, J. W. (1995). American Indians in a new world. In *Cultural awareness in the human services: A multi-ethnic approach.* Boston: Allyn and Bacon.

> **Comprehensive chapter covering the nature of culture, definition of Indian, genesis of using blood quantum as a means of tribal inclusion, and origins of stereotypes of native people. The author notes the vast diversity of native peoples in North America, explains the treaty relationship between the federal government and American Indian nations, and discusses policies which have served to disempower indigenous peoples to this day. Special challenges to social workers in native communities include those of language, belief, geography, complex variations in family structure, and degree of acculturation. Social problems of alcoholism, suicide, and the like pose additional problems. The article also contains a table of contrasts between Anglo and native culture, and explores ways in which social workers can develop cultural competence to work with Indian people.**

Hamilton, C. (1913). *Cry of the thunderbird: The American Indian's own story.* Norman, OK: University of Oklahoma Press.

Hanson, W. D. (1980). *The urban Indian.* San Francisco: San Francisco State University.

> **This is a collection of articles on urban American Indians in the San Francisco area. Topics include social development, grief counseling, psychotherapy, women, sexuality, and older persons.**

Hirschfelder, A., & Montano, M. K. (1993). *The Native American almanac: A portrait of Native America today*. New York: Prentice-Hall.

> The authors provide a history of American Indian relationships with the federal government, its policies, treaties, laws, and court decisions, the BIA, and tribal governments, as well as examining contemporary legal and social issues faced by native peoples in the U.S. The book also includes information on education, religion, famous persons, employment, lists of reservations and tribes, and a historical chronology.

In whose honor: Indian mascots and nicknames in sports [VHS]. (1996). (Available from Jay Rosenstein, Box 2483, Champaign, IL)

> An advocate fights stereotypes on the University of Illinois campus.

Department of Indian Affairs and Northern Development. (1995). *Indian register population by sex and residence*. Ottawa, Canada: Author.

> This document gives a detailed breakdown of information on Canadian tribal groups.

Johnson, B. B. (1982). American Indian jurisdiction as a policy issue. *Social Work, 27*, 31-37.

> The author gives a summary of federal policies and issues vis-a-vis Native American tribes.

Johnson, L. L. (1984). Non-metropolitan service delivery revisited: Insights from a dozen years of participant observation. *Human Services in the Rural Environment, 9*(2), 21-25.

> This is a look at service delivery in small town, rural, and reservation settings.

Katz, W. L. (1986). *Black Indians: A hidden heritage*. New York: Atheneum.

> This book examines one of the little-known aspects of American history: the relationship between indigenous Americans and African-Americans.

LaFromboise, T. (1988). American Indian mental health policy. *American Psychologist, 43*(5), 388-397

Lipsyte, R. (1995, November 26). The invisible nations in plain sight. *New York Times*, p. 13-1.

> The author reports on social and legal challenges facing the 30,000 to 40,000 Native Americans living in New York City.

Little Bear, L., Boldt, M., & Long, J. A. (1984). *Pathways to self-determination: Canadian Indians and the Canadian state*. Toronto, Canada: University of Toronto Press.

Little Eagle, A. (1993, February 11). Ten years later: Shannon still poorest county in the nation. *Indian Country Today*.

Littlefield, D. (1977). *Africans and Seminoles: From removal to emancipation*. Westport, CT: Greenwood.

Lockhart, A., & McCaskill, D. (1986). Toward an integrated, community-based partnership model of native development and training: a case study in process. *The Canadian Journal of Native Studies, 6*(2), 159-172.

Mala, T. A. (1985). Alaska Native grass roots movement: Problem solving utilizing indigenous values. *Arctic Medical Research, 40*(2), 84-91.

Mercredi, O., & Turpel, M. E. (1994). *In the rapids: Navigating the future of First Nations.* Toronto, Canada: Penguin Books.

> **This is an outline of the movement of First Nations of Canada toward developing an Assembly of First Nations and seeking rights for indigenous peoples. The author looks at policies on native identity, politics, and issues facing First Nations peoples around the globe.**

Nabokov, P. (Ed.). (1991). *Native American testimony: A chronicle of Indian-White relations from prophecy to the present, 1492-1992.* New York; Viking Press.

> **Documents, accounts, biographies, newspapers, interviews, diaries and letters tell the story of American Indians since the European invasion.**

Nagel, J., & Snipp, C. M. (1993). Ethnic reorganization: American Indian social, economic, political and cultural strategies for survival. *Ethnic and Racial Studies, 16*(2), 203-235.

> **This article explores what happens when minority and majority populations are in contact — annihilation, assimilation, amalgamation, and accommodation. All of these consequences have characterized Indian-White relations. A fifth process, ethnic reorganization, is identified by the authors as occurring when a minority is reorganized in terms of its social structures, group boundaries, or the like in response to the impact of the dominant culture.**

Smith, D. (1993). *The seventh fire: The struggle for aboriginal government.* Toronto, Canada: Key Porter Books.

Smith, D. M. (1998). Interorganizational collaboration: A cautionary note for tribal health nurses. *Public Health Nursing, 15*(2), 131-135.

> **Tribes are assuming more control of health care services and establishing collaborative relationships for health care. This article focuses on nursing, but has general implications for health and human services workers.**

Stauss, J. H., Chadwick, B., Bahr, H. M., & Halverson, L. K. (1979). An experimental outreach legal aid program for an urban Native American population utilizing legal paraprofessionals. *Human Organization, 38*(4), 386-394.

Taylor, M. J. (1996). Effects of a two-parent welfare program: Factors associated with time to employment. *Research on Social Work Practice, 6*(3), 277-291.

Weaver, H. N. (1998). Indigenous peoples in a multicultural society: Unique issues for the human services. *Social Work, 43*, 203-211.

> **Native peoples have a unique status in the U. S. The author stresses that social service workers need to be aware of issues such as historic trauma and moral and legal obligations of the federal and state government to tribes.**

Weaver, H. N. (1999). Assessing the needs of Native American communities: A northeastern example. *Evaluation and Program Planning: an International Journal, 22*(2), 155-161.

Weaver, H. N. (2000). Culture and professional education: The experiences of Native American social workers. *Journal of Social Work Education*, 36, 415-429.

Weaver, H. N. (in press). Activism and American Indian issues: Opportunities and roles for social workers. *Journal of Progressive Human Services*.

Wilkins, D. E. (1993). Modernization, colonialism, dependency: How appropriate are these models for providing an explanation of North American Indian underdevelopment? *Ethnic and Racial Studies, 16*(3), 390-419.

> **This article evaluates third world models of development. It begins with an overview of the political and legal status of tribes and their status vis-a-vis the United States, then summarizes each model with an evaluation of the literature. The author emphasizes that no theoretical perspective explains every tribal situation, and there is need for research that takes into account the situation of tribes in a democracy.**

Wilkinson, G. T. (1980). On assisting Indian people. *Social Casework, 61*(8), 453-456.

Yellow Bird, M. (1999). Indian, American Indian, and Native Americans: Counterfeit identities. *Winds of Change: A Magazine for American Indian Education and Opportunity, 14* (1), 86.

> **In this critical essay, the author argues that Indian, American Indian, and Native American are inaccurate, confusing, and colonized identities. The author maintains that the continued use of these terms is oppressive and that the scholarship about First Nations peoples must be decolonized through the use of more empowering descriptors.**

Yellow Bird, M. J. (in press). What we want to be called: Indigenous perspectives on racial and ethnic identity labels. *American Indian Quarterly*.

> **Identity politics is a very critical issue for First Nations peoples. In this article, indigenous peoples in academia present their opinions on the current racial labels that are applied to aboriginal peoples in the United States and Canada. Opinions indicate that the respondents have a very high level of consciousness concerning the labels used to identify indigenous peoples and what they want to be called is a very important issue. The article examines how current labels such as "Indian," "American Indian," and "Native American" affect self-definition and identity, institutional oppression, social interaction, and group solidity among indigenous peoples.**

PRACTICE

Baker, C. C. (1981). *A resource guide to work with American Indian and Spanish-speaking clients.* New Orleans, LA: Tulane University, School of Social Work.

Brendtro, L. K., & Brokenleg, M. (1993). Beyond the curriculum of control. *Journal of Emotional and Behavioral Problems, 1*(4), 5-11.

The authors discuss the use of an empowerment model within a native paradigm to treat behavior problems.

Broken Nose, M. A. (1992). Working with the Oglala Lakota: An outsider's perspective. *Families in Society: The Journal of Contemporary Human Services,* June, 380-384.

Canda, E. R., & Yellow Bird, M. J. (1997). Another view, cultural strengths are crucial. *Families in Society: The Journal of Contemporary Human Services, 78* (3), 248.

The entire community is the most effective clinic. This article provides a short commentary on how cultural strengths are critical in the development of culturally competent strategies for AOD abuse treatment.

DuBray, W. H. (1993). *Human Services and American Indians.* Minneapolis, MN: West Publishing.

Edwards, D. E. (1984). Group work practice with American Indians. *Social Work with Groups, 7*(3), 7-21.

Edwards, E. D., & Edwards, M. E. (1980). American Indians: Working with individuals and groups. *Social Casework, 61*(8), 498-506.

Family Service Association of America. (1980). Phoenix from the flame: The American Indian [Special Issue]. *Social Casework, 61*(8).

Good, B. J., & Good, M. D. (1986). The cultural context of diagnosis and therapy: A view from medical anthropology. In M. R. Miranda & H. L. Kitano (Eds.), *Mental health research and practice in minority communities: Development of a culturally sensitive training programs* (pp. 1-27). Rockville, MD: National Institutes of Mental Health. (ERIC Document Reproduction Service No. ED 278 754).

Hanson, W. D., & Eisenbrise, M. D. (1982). *Social work methods of intervention with American Indians.* San Francisco: San Francisco State University. (ERIC Document Reproduction Service No. ED 231 590).

Healing the hurts [VHS]. (1989). (Available from Four Worlds Development Project, Lethbirdge, Canada)

A ceremony is held at Alkali Lake to heal the trauma of residential boarding school experience.

Heinrich, R. K., Corine, J. L., & Thomas, K. R. (1990). Counseling Native Americans. *Journal of Counseling and Development, 69*(2), 128-133.

Kaplan, B., & Johnson, D. (1964). The social meaning of Navajo psychopathology and psychotherapy. In A. Kiev (Ed.), *Magic, faith and healing* (pp. 203 – 229). Glencoe, NY: Free Press.

LaFromboise, T. D., & Dixon, D. N. (1981). American Indian perceptions of trustworthiness in a counseling interview. *Journal of Counseling Psychology, 28*(2), 165-169.

Lewis, R. G. (1980). Cultural perspective on treatment modalities with Native Americans. In M. Bloom (Ed.), *Life span development* (pp. 434-441). New York: MacMillan.

> The healing power of nature, natural helping systems, and use of self-help groups are discussed as modalities effective in treating emotional and mental disorders among Native American peoples.

Lewis, R. G., & Ho, M. K. (1975). Social work with Native Americans. *Social Work, 20,* 379-382.

Littrell, M. A., & Littrell, J. M. (1983). Counselor dress cues: Evaluations by American Indians and Caucasians. *Journal of Cross-Cultural Psychology, 14*(1), 109-121.

Thompson, C. A. (1978/1979). Native American awareness: An institutional response. *Interchange, 9*(1), 45-55.

Trimble, J. E., & Fleming, C. M. (1989). Providing counseling services for Native American Indians: Client, counselor and community characteristics. In P. B. Pedersen, J. G. Draguna, & W. G. Loner (Eds.), *Counseling across cultures* (pp. 177-204). Honolulu, HI: University of Hawaii Press.

Weaver, H. N. (1997). Which canoe are you in? A view from a First Nations person. *Reflections: Narratives of Professional Helping, A Journal for the Helping Professions, 4*(3), 12-17.

Weaver, H. N. (1999). Indigenous peoples and the social work profession: Defining culturally competent services. *Social Work, 44,* 217-225.

Yellow Bird, M. J. (in press). Critical values and First Nations peoples. In R. Fong & S. Furuto (Eds.), *Cultural competent social work practice: Practice skills, interventions, and evaluation.* New York: Longman Press.

> This article discusses several key values of First Nations peoples. The first part provides a brief definition of indigenous peoples and examines the effects of European American colonialism on the values of these groups. The second part concentrates on macro values critical to First Nations peoples' empowerment and makes suggestions for culturally competent and justice-oriented social work practice.

Yellow Bird, M. J., & Chenault, V. (1999). The role of social work in advancing indigenous education: Obstacles and promises in empowerment-oriented social work practice. In K. Swisher & J. Tippeconnic (Eds.), *Next steps: Research and practice to advance Indian education* (pp. 201-235). (ERIC Document Reproduction Service No. ED 427922).

> The professional mission of social work and the roles of the social worker can advance the practice of indigenous peoples' education. Empowerment-oriented social work practices illustrate how this is possible. To create change, educators and social workers must develop strong collaborative relationships with social workers. This article examines several ways educators and social workers can use empowerment-oriented social work practice to improve the education of First Nations students. First, it examines historical and structural obstacles to advancing indigenous peoples' education. Second, it discusses how the professional behavior, education, and roles of social workers can help address several micro and macro issues preventing the advancement of First Nations education.

RESEARCH

Barnsley, J., & Ellis, D. (1992). *Research for change; Participatory action for community groups.* Vancouver, Canada: The Women's Research Centre.

Cook, L. S., & DeMange, B. P. (1995). Gaining access to Native American cultures by non-Native American nursing researchers. *Nursing Forum, 30*(1), 5-10.

> This article offers suggestions for non-natives who wish to access American Indian tribes for research purposes. It also discusses the barriers to American Indian participation in research.

Gilliard, F. D., Mahler, R., & Davis, S. M. (1998). Health-related quality of life for rural American Indians in New Mexico. *Ethnicity and Health, 3*(3), 223-229.

> This telephone survey of over 600 American Indians is considered by the authors to be an efficient tool for data collection with this population. Over half reported their health to be representative of that of the rural American Indian population reported in the 1990 census. See Pearson et al., for another perspective on the use of the telephone for data collection in this population.

LaFromboise, T. D., & Plake, B. S. (1984). A model for the systematic review of mental health research: American Indian family, a case in point. *White Cloud Journal of American Indian Mental Health, 3*(3), 44-52.

> A model is proposed for conducting research and/or training with native researchers in their communities.

Macaulay, A. C., Delormier, T., McComber, A. M., Cross, E. J., Potvin, L. P., Paradis, G., Kirby, R. L., Sadd-Haddad, C., & Desrosiers, S. (1998). Participatory research with a native community of Kahnawake creates innovative code of research ethics. *Canadian Journal of Public Health, 89*(2), 105-108.

> Ethical guidelines for participatory research were developed from a project with a Canadian First Nations community. Community control of data and issues of publication are among topics discussed.

Norton, I. M., & Manson, S. M. (1996). Research in American Indian and Alaska Native communities: Navigating the cultural universe of values and process. *Journal of Consulting and Clinical Psychology, 64*(5), 55-63.

> The authors discuss how native communities present challenges to the researcher in terms of access and differing beliefs about the goals and purposes of research.

Novins, D. K., Bechtold, D. W., Sack, W., Thompson, J., Carter, D. R., & Manson, S. M. (1997). The DSM-IV outline for cultural formulation: A critical demonstration with American Indian children. *Journal of the American Academy of Child and Adolescent Psychiatry, 36*(9), 1244-1251.

> This article provides information on cultural formulation specific to American Indian children and adolescents.

Oesterhold, J. R., & Haber, J. R. (1997). Acceptability of the Conner's Parent Rating Scale and Child Behavior Checklist to Dakotan/Lakotan Parents. *Journal of the American Academy of Child and Adolescent Psychiatry, 36*(1), 55-64.

Pearson, D., Chaedle, A., Wagner, E., Tonsberg, R., & Psaty, B. M. (1994). Differences in sociodemographics, health status, and lifestyle characteristics among American Indians by telephone coverage. *Preventive Medicine, 23*(4). 461-464.

> **This study of over 400 respondents shows that those who lacked phones also had poorer health status, less healthy lifestyles, less likelihood of employment, lower educational status, and lower income. Researchers who use telephone surveys with reservation residents need to be aware that many do not have phones and will not be included in studies, thus skewing findings. (See Gilliard in "Families" for a different perspective on use of telephone surveys in this population.)**

Ryan, R. A., & Spence, J. D. (1978). Indian mental health research: Local control and cultural sensitivity. *White Cloud Journal of American Indian Health, 1*(1), 15-18.

> **The authors suggest that factors affecting the failure of mental health research to help native peoples is due to lack of relevancy, faulty communication, and lack of fit between instruments and native culture. Non-natives fail to understand values, customs, language, and culture of First Nations peoples.**

Troimble, J. E. (1977). The sojourner in the American Indian community: Methodological issues and concerns. *Journal of Social Issues, 33*(4), 159-174.

> **This article states that research has done little to help develop programs or solve problems for indigenous communities. Research is often from a non-Native framework and the methods, procedures, and findings do not fit the culture. Steps are given for conducting relevant and appropriate research.**

Weaver, H. N. (1997). The challenges of research in Native American communities: Incorporating principles of cultural competence. *Journal of Social Services Research, 23*(2), 1-15.

> **Weaver discusses access to American Indian communities and the conduct of culturally appropriate research.**

White Deer of Autumn, & Begay, S. W. (1992). *The Native American book of life* [Volume 2 of *Native peoples Native ways*]. Hillsboro, OR: Beyond Words Publishing.

> **This is about children's lives and the importance of children to traditional peoples.**

SEXUAL ORIENTATION (GAY, LESBIAN, BISEXUAL, TRANSEXUAL, TRANSGENDERED)

Allen, P. G. (1981). Lesbians in American Indian cultures. *Conditions, 7*(1), 67-87.

Blackwood, E. (1984). Sexuality and gender in certain Native American tribes: The case of cross-gender females. *Signs: A Journal of Women in Culture and Society, 10*(3), 27-43.

Brown, L. (1997). Women and men, not-men, not-women, lesbians and gays: American Indian gender style alternatives. In L. Brown (Ed.), *Two spirit people: American Indian lesbian women and gay men* (pp. 5-21). New York: Harrington Park Press.

Brown, L. B. (Ed.). (1997). *Two spirit people: American Indian lesbian women and gay men.* New York: Harrington Park Press. (Originally published as *Journal of Gay and Lesbian Social Services, 6* (2), 1997).

This is a comprehensive collection of articles on gay, lesbian, bisexual and transgendered individuals and the issues they encounter as members of First Nations societies. In general, North American native peoples have not only exhibited attitudes of tolerance and acceptance, but also have provided positive social roles for those with differing sexual orientations.

Crow, L., Wright, J. A., & Brown, L. B. (1997). Gender selection in two American Indian tribes. In L. Brown (Ed.), *Two spirit people: American Indian lesbian women and gay men* (pp. 21-29). New York: Harrington Park Press.

Grahn, J. (1986). Strange country this: Lesbianism and North American Indian tribes. *Journal of Homosexuality, 12*(3/4), 43-57.

Honored by the moon [VHS]. (1989). (Available from Women Make Movies, New York)

This film looks at Native American gays and lesbians, and their role in the tribal societies to which they belong. This particular video focuses primarily on the status and role of lesbian women.

Jacobs, M. A., & Brown, L. B. (1997). American Indian lesbians and gays: An exploratory study. In L. Brown (Ed.), *Two spirit people: American Indian lesbian women and gay men* (pp. 29-42). New York: Harrington Park Press.

Roscoe, W. (1989). Bibliography of Berdache and alternative gender roles among North American Indians. *Journal of Homosexuality, 14,*(3-4), 81-171.

Saewyc, E. M., Skay, C. L., Bearinger, L. H., Blum, R. W., & Resnick, M. D. (1998). Sexual orientation, sexual behavior, and pregnancy among American Indian adolescents. *Journal of Adolescent Health, 23*(4), 238-247.

In this sample of over 2,000 males and 1,700 females, American Indian adolescents have higher rates of pregnancy than do other groups of teens, as well as higher numbers individuals identifying as gay, lesbian, or bisexual.

Walters, K. (1997). Urban lesbian and gay American Indian identity: Implications for mental health service delivery. In L. Brown (Ed.), *Two spirit people: American Indian lesbian women and gay men* (pp. 43-66). New York: Harrington Park Press.

Wright, J. A., Lopez, M. A., & Zumwalt, L. L. (1997). That's what they say: The implications of American Indian gay and lesbian literature for social service workers. In L. Brown (Ed.), *Two spirit people: American Indian lesbian women and gay men* (pp. 67-84). New York: Harrington Park Press.

SPIRITUALITY AND RELIGION

Bahr, D. (1991). Interpreting sacramental systems: The Midewiwin and the Wi:gita. *Wicazo SA Review, 7*(2), 18-25.

Benally, H. J. (1992). Spiritual knowledge for a secular society: Traditional Navajo spirituality offers lessons for the nation. *Tribal College Journal of American Higher Education, 3*(4), 19-22.

Brant, C. C. (1990). Native ethics and rules of behavior. *Canadian Journal of Psychiatry, 35*(6), 534-539.

Canda, E. R., & Yellow Bird, M. J. (1996). Cross-tradition borrowing of spiritual practices in social work settings. *Society for Spirituality and Social Work Newsletter, 3*(1), 1, 7.

> **Spirituality cannot be divorced from politics and justice concerns, especially with regard to First Nations peoples, without abuse, intentional or unintentional. This article discusses the politics of borrowing spiritual beliefs and activities from First Nations peoples and provides insights for social workers to consider before borrowing any First Nations spiritual practices.**

Cianci, D., & Nadon, S. (1987). *Walking the medicine wheel path in daylight: An exploration of the medicine wheel teachings on human relationships.* Owen, Ontario: Maplestone Press.

Deloria, V., Jr. (1992). Secularism, civil religion, and the religious freedom of American Indians. *American Indian Culture and Research Journal, 16*(2), 9-20.

Deloria, V., Jr. (1994). *God is red: A Native view of religion.* Golden, CO: Fulcrum Press.

DeMallia, R. J., & Parks, D. R. (1987). *Sioux Indian religion.* Norman, OK: University of Oklahoma Press.

Griffin-Pierce, T. (1988). Cosmological order as a model of Navajo philosophy. *American Indian Culture and Research Journal, 12*(4), 1-15.

Lame Deer, J., & Erodes, R. (1972). *Lame Deer, seeker of visions: The life of a Sioux medicine man.* New York: Touchstone/Simon and Schuster.

Lewis, J. R. (1988). Shamans and prophets: Continuities and discontinuities in Native American new religions. *American Indian Quarterly, 12*(3), 221-228.

Loftin, J. D. (1989). Anglo-American jurisprudence and the Native American tribal quest for religious freedom. *American Indian Culture and Research Journal, 13*(1), 1-52.

Medicine people: Teaching and healing [VHS]. (1988). (Available from the Native American Research and Training Center, Tucson, AZ)

Medicine woman, medicine man: Traditional holistic medicine in middle America [VHS]. (1985). (Available from Singer-Sharrette Productions, Rochester MI)

Moore, S. C. (1991). Reflections on the elusive promise of religious freedom for the Native American church. *Wicazo SA Review, 7*(1), 42-50.

Raymond, C. (1990). Reburial of Indian remains stimulates studies, friction among scholars. *Chronicle of Higher Education, 37*(5), 12-13.

Sanborn, G. (1990). Unfencing the range: History, identity, property and apocalypse in "Lame Deer Seeker of Visions." *American Indian Culture and Research Journal, 14*(4), 39-57.

Steinmetz, P. B. (1984). The sacred pipe in American Indian religions. *American Indian Culture and Research Journal, 14*(4), 39-57.

Steinmetz, P. B. (1990). *Pipe, Bible and peyote among the Oglala Lakota. A study in religious identity* (Rev. ed.). Knoxville, TN: University of Tennessee Press.

The spirit world. (1992). Alexandria, VA: Time-Life Books.

Traditional spiritual beliefs and ceremonies are described among a number of tribes, with photographs, drawings, and maps.

Willard, W. (1991). The first amendment, Anglo-conformity, and American Indian religious freedom. *Wicazo SA Review, 7*(1), 25-41.

Yellow Bird, M. J. (1995). Spirituality in First Nations story telling: A Sahnish-Hidatsa approach to narrative. *Reflections: Narratives of Professional Helping, A Journal for the Helping Professions, 1*(4), 65-72.

Storytelling is one of the most important ways to define and give meaning to the spirituality of First Nations peoples. In this article the author shares four aspects of storytelling that supports the spirituality of First Nations peoples. The narratives of the author's village attest to the pain, loss, resiliency, hope, and humanity that is found among his peoples.

SUICIDE

Colorado, P. (1992). Aboriginal suicide in British Columbia: An overview. *Canada's Mental Health, 40*(3), 19-23.

Echo Hawk, M. (1997). Suicide: The scourge of Native American people. *Suicide and Life-Threatening Behavior, 27*(1), 60-67.

This author argues that the higher rate of suicide among Native Americans may in part be explained by the impact of the European invasion.

Fox, J. , Manitowabi, D., & Ward, J. A. (1984). An Indian community with a high suicide rate: Five years after. *Canadian Journal of Psychiatry, 29*(5), 425-427.

Isaacs, S., Keogh, S., Menard, C., & Hockin. J. (1998). Suicide in the Northwest Territories: A descriptive view. *Chronic Diseases in Canada, 19*(4), 152-156.

This article shows that the most significant factors associated with suicide among Inuit people of the Northwest Territories include problems with relationships and having been charged with illegal activity in the criminal justice system.

Keane, E. M., Dick, R. W., Bechtold, D. W., & Manson, S. M. (1996). Predictive and concurrent validity of the Suicidal Ideation Questionnaire among American Indian adolescents. *Journal of Abnormal Child Psychology, 24*(6), 735-747.

This instrument appears to predict future suicide attempts among American Indian adolescents.

Kettl, P. (1998). Alaska Native suicide: Lessons for elder suicide. *International Psychogeriatrics, 10*(2), 205-211.

Suicide rates among Alaska Native Elders are low compared to the general population. The authors suggest that this is due to cultural teachings, even in times of change, such as the Alaska oil boom. Social factors do appear to influence suicide rates, however, both positively and negatively.

LaFromboise, T., & Howard-Pitney, B. (1995). The Zuni life-skills development curriculum: Description and evaluation of a suicide prevention program. *Journal of Counseling Psychology, 42*(4), 479-486.

This article describes a model for suicide prevention, using behavioral and cognitive correlates of suicide.

Lester, D. (1995). Social correlates of American Indian suicide and homicide rates. *American Indian and Alaska Native Mental Health Research, 6*(3), 46-55.

This article explores correlates of suicide and homicide among both native and white populations.

Long, K. (1986). Suicide intervention and prevention with Indian adolescents. *Issues in Mental Health Nursing, 8*(3), 247-253.

Mock, D. C., Grossman, D., Mulder, D., Stewart, C., & Koepsell, T. S. (1996). Health care utilization as a marker for suicidal behavior on an American Indian reservation. *Journal of General Internal Medicine, 11*(9), 519-524.

This longitudinal study of completed and attempted suicides on a Plains Indian reservation assesses utilization of health services preceding the event. The results indicate that attempters were more likely than controls to have had prior psychological and interpersonal problems, suggesting a need for improved detection and intervention as well as an assessment of the value of community outreach efforts.

Norton, G. R., Rockman, G., Luy, B., & Marion, T. (1993). Suicide, chemical abuse, and panic attacks: A preliminary report. *Behavior Research and Therapy, 3*(1), 37-40.

What happened to Mike? American Indian youth and suicide [VHS]. (1990). (Available from the University of New Mexico Center for Indian Youth Program Development , Albuquerque, NM)

A male high school senior attempts suicide. This film is designed to spark discussion.

URBAN ISSUES

Hanson, W. D. (1980). *The urban Indian.* San Francisco: San Francisco State University.

> This is a collection of articles on urban American Indians in the San Francisco area. Topics include social development, grief counseling, psychotherapy, women, sexuality, and older persons.

Hill, T. W. (1980). Life styles and drinking patterns of urban Indians. *Journal of Drug Issues*, 3(2), 257-272.

Holden, G., Moncher, M. S., Gordon, A., & Schinke, S. P. (1990). Avoidable mortality risks and cultural identification among urban Native American youths. *Journal of Adolescent Health Care,* 288-290.

Kramer, B. J. (1992). Health and aging of urban American Indians. *Western Journal of Medicine, 157*(3), 281-285.

> Half of American Indians live off the reserve, but research on their health status is limited. Native people living in urban areas are not eligible for IHS services, but are nonetheless at high risk for many health problems. This article identifies barriers that interfere with access to health care, particularly for older persons, and the authors stress that it is possible to provide better access to services for older native people.

Sugarman, J. R., Brenneman, G., LaRoque, W., Warren, C. W., & Goldberg, H. L. (1994). The urban American Indian oversample in the 1988 National Maternal and Infant Health Survey. *Public Health Reports, 109*(2), 243-250.

> Two-thirds of American Indian and Alaska natives live in urban settings, and yet the authors show that there is little information about maternal-child health risk factors in this population. Poverty, difficulty and delays in obtaining prenatal care, as well as lack of health coverage were also reported as more frequent among American Indians.

Westerfelt, A., & Yellow Bird, M. (1999). Homeless and indigenous in Minneapolis. *Journal of Human Behavior in the Social Environment, 2*(1/2), 145-162.

> Indigenous peoples are over-represented in the homeless population. This article examines the extent to which homelessness and some of its possible antecedents and consequences differ for indigenous peoples and majority whites residing in the city of Minneapolis. Based upon empirical data, the authors conclude that being homeless and indigenous in Minneapolis is a significantly different experience for this group than it is for majority whites.

VETERANS

Johnson, D. (1994). Stress, depression, substance abuse, and racism. *American Indian and Alaska Native Mental Health Research, 6*(1), 29-33.

> The author states that Indian veterans have cultural and identity problems and issues of self-esteem related to stress, depression, drug-alcohol abuse, and racism.

Kasprow, W. J., & Rosenheck, R. (1998). Substance abuse and psychiatric problems of homeless Native American veterans. *Psychiatric Services, 49*(3), 345-350.

> **Higher rates of homelessness, alcohol dependence, hospitalization, and intoxication characterize American Indian veterans compared with other minority groups.**

Silver, S. (1994). Lessons from child of water. *American Indian and Alaska Native Mental Health Research, 6*(1), 4-17.

> **This article is about treating post-traumatic stress disorder among native veterans.**

Walker, R. D., Howard, M. O., Anderson, B., & Lambert, M. D. (1994). Substance dependent American Indian veterans: A national evaluation. *Public Health Reports, 109*(2), 235-242.

> **This survey of over 3,000 American Indian veterans shows higher rates of substance abuse than in the general population. Reasons for this anomaly are discussed.**

VOCATIONAL REHABILITATION AND WORK

D'Alonzo, B. (1996). American Indian vocational rehabilitation services: A unique project. *American Rehabilitation, 22*(1), 20-26.

> **This article describes a rehabilitation project for 131 participants using professionals fluent in the native language.**

Locust, C., & Lang, J. (1996). Walking in two worlds: Native Americans and the system. *American Rehabilitation, 22*(2), 184-188.

> **The authors discuss their findings that motivation for vocational rehabilitation services is associated with the level of the individual's acculturation. An individual's definition of work varies according to his or her culture. The authors discuss the definition and meaning of work in different cultures.**

Miller, D. L., & Joe, J. R. (1993). Employment barriers and work motivation for Navajo rehabilitation clients. *International Journal of Rehabilitation Research, 16*(2), 107-117.

> **The authors make suggestions for vocational rehabilitation counselors.**

Ramasamy, R. (1996). Post-high school employment: A follow-up of Apache Native American youth. *Journal of Learning Disabilities, 29*(2), 174-179.

Taylor, M. J. (1996). Effects of a two-parent welfare program: Factors associated with time to employment. *Research on Social Work Practice, 6*(3), 277-291.

WOMEN

Ahenakew, F., & Wolfart, H. C. (1992). *Our grandmothers' lives as told in their words.* Saskatoon, Canada: Fifth House Publishers.

Allen, P. G. (1986). *The sacred hoop: Recovering the feminine in American Indian traditions.* Boston: Beacon Press.

Allen, P. G. (1991). *Grandmothers of the light: A medicine woman's sourcebook.* Boston: Beacon Press.

Bataille, G. M., & Sands, K. M. (1984). *American Indian women, telling their lives.* London: University of Nebraska Press.

Brafford, C. J., & Laine, T. (1992). *Dancing colors: Paths of Native American women.* San Francisco: Chronicle Books.

> **The authors provide color photographs of artifacts that were part of traditional life for native women as they tell four legends that demonstrate women's roles and status in traditional culture. The book includes a bibliography.**

Chesler, M. A. (1991). Participatory action research with self-help groups: An alternative paradigm for inquiry and action. *American Journal of Community Psychology, 19*(5), 757-768.

Goodluck, C. (1998). *Understanding Navajo ethnic identity: Weaving the meaning through the voices of young girls.* Unpublished doctoral dissertation, University of Denver.

Green, R. (1983). *Native American women: A contextual bibliography.* Bloomington, IN: Indiana University Press.

Her give-away: A spiritual journal [VHS]. (1987). (Available from Women Make Movies, New York)

> **This film shows how a native woman copes with her diagnosis of AIDS through her spirituality.**

Hodge, F. S., Fredericks, L., & Rodriquez, B. (1996). American Indian women's Talking Circle: A cervical cancer screening and prevention project. *Cancer, 78* (suppl. 7), 1592-1597.

> **American Indian women have higher rates of mortality as a result of cervical cancer than do other groups. This screening program made use of the Talking Circle and traditional American Indian stories to provide education and encourage compliance. The study used a sample of 400 women aged 18 and older and responses to this approach were deemed favorable by the researchers.**

Ikajurti: The helper: Midwifery in the Canadian Arctic [VHS]. (1990). (Available from Inuit Broadcasting Corporation and Paktutit Womens' Association, Ottawa, Canada)

> **This film demonstrates that there is a need for midwives in remote Inuit communities where access to hospitals is difficult. Consider for HBSE/child development classes.**

Johnston, C. R. (1996). In the white woman's image? Resistance, transformation, and identity in recent Native American women's history. *Journal of Women's History, 8*(3), 205-216.

Koehler, L. (1982). Native women of the Americas: A bibliography [Special Issue]. *Frontiers, 6*(4).

Kvigne, V. L., Bull, L. B., Welty, T. K., Leonardson, G. R., & Lacina, L. (1998). Relationship of prenatal alcohol use with maternal and prenatal factors in American Indian women. *Social Biology, 45*(3/4), 214-222.

> **Patterns of prenatal drinking and access to transportation correlate with other risk factors.**

Lake, R. G. (1983). Shamanism in northwestern California: A female perspective on sickness, healing and health. *White Cloud Journal of American Indian Mental Health, 3*(1), 31-42.

Light, L., & Kleiber, N. (1981). Interactive research in a feminist setting: The Vancouver Women's Health Collective. In D. Messerschmidt, (Ed.), *Anthropologists at home in North America* (pp. 167-182). London: Cambridge University Press.

Luchetti, C., & Olwell, C. (1982). *Women of the West.* St. George, UT: Antelope Island Press.

Census material and original documents give information about women in the West, including a section on women of color. This book also contains a chronology.

Lytle, L. J., Bakken, L., & Romig, C. (1991). Adolescent female identity development. *Sex Roles, 37*(3-4), 175-185.

This study of 600 youngsters includes an American Indian cohort. The authors sought to determine whether there were gender specific differences in identity development among adolescent males and females, and found there was.

Muraga, C., & Anzaldua, G. (Eds). (1983). Native American women. In *This bridge called my back: Writings by radical women of color.* New York: Kitchen Table /Women of Color Press.

Napholtz, L. (1995). Mental health and American Indian women's multiple roles. *American Indian and Alaska Native Mental Health Research, 6*(2), 57-75.

This articles explores sex roles and psychological well-being among 148 native working women.

Napier, L. A. (1995). Educational profiles of nine gifted American Indian women and their own stories about wanting to lead. *Roeper Review, 18*(1), 38-44.

This is a study of nine women in the American Indian doctoral leadership program at Pennsylvania State University.

Niethammer, C. (1977). *Daughters of the earth: The lives and legends of American Indian women.* New York: Macmillan.

Topics discussed in this book include women and marriage, birth, growing-up, rites of passage ceremonies, economics, and war.

Osburn, K. M. B. (1997). To build up the morals of the tribe: Southern Ute women's sexual behavior and the Office of Indian Affairs, 1895-1932. *Journal of Women's History, 9*(3), 10-27.

Silman, J. (1987). *Enough is enough: Aboriginal women speak out.* Toronto, Canada: The Women's Press.

INTERNET RESOURCES

Author's note: Citations on the Internet are constantly changing. These were current at the time of compilation, but it is likely there have been numerous deletions and changes. Users are encouraged to pursue topics of interest on search engines and to bookmark various sites relevant to their work. Agencies such as SAMSHA, NIMH, and others offer useful information or fund centers focused on First Nations peoples and issues.

http://www.aaip.com/tradmed

> Association of American Indian Physicians website; information on traditional medicine is included.

http://www.aoa.gov/ain/default.htm

> Information on Native American seniors from the U.S. Administration on Aging.

http://www.aoa.gov/factsheets/natams.html

> General information on older American Indians and programs for Alaska Natives, native Hawaiians, and Native Americans. Federal interagency task force, Colorado, and North Dakota program sites.

http://www.sc.edu/swan/topics.html

> University of South Carolina School of Social Work. Multiple links to other sites, including Native America. Also includes social work bulletin boards, and discussion groups.

http://www.ankn.uaf.edu/

> The Native knowledge network.

http://www.bluecloud.org/25.html

> The American Indian Cultural Center short bibliography on American Indians.

http://bos-fe6-1.bos.lycos.com/wguide/wire/wire_94046194_83233-3_1.html.

> The Pan American Indian website.

http://www.cumber.edu/personal/jburch/burch.html

> A web guide to legal, anthropological, and other areas relevant to Native American interests.

http://www.first-nation.com/

> The seven teachings in story and biography.

http://www.hanksville.org/NAresources/NAresourcestxt.html

> Links to American Indian resources on the web.

http://nmhwww.si.edu/anthro/outreach/Indbibl/bibliogr.html

> The Smithsonian anthropology outreach office with a bibliography for K–12 that contains over 800 listings.

http://sorrel.humboldt.edu/~nasp/history.html

> A Native history website.

http://www.uncg.edu/edu/ericcass/diverse/ethnic/natv_toc.htm

> A website on Indians in higher education, including rates of graduation and related information.

http://www.webdb.nyu.edu/sociallink/smenu.cgi?cid+405

> Social work diversity: Native American. This site includes related resources by Gary Holden.

hattp://www.yak.net/third/Ref/comments.html#epsBodyCmnt

> A website on transgender and spirituality.

www.nativeweb.org

> News and resources for indigenous peoples around the world.

www.omhrc.gov

> Office of Minority Health Resource Center.

doi.gov.bia/childwe~2htm

> Social service website of Department of the Interior.

doi.gov/bia/otshome.htm

> Office of tribal services, with information on alcohol, research, child abuse, labor, etc.

dbi.gov/bia/child/childprt.html

> Indian child protection home page.

http://indy4.fdl.cc.mn.us/!isk/

> A website from the American Indian quarterly, about culture and education, that is no longer maintained

http://www.matgicnet.net/~itms/IHSSterilizationRef.html

> Indian Health service policy on sterilization, 1972-1976

http://www.ruralinstitute.umt.edu/rtcrural/Indian/Indian/Indian_choices.htm

> A website on disabilities from the Rural Institute, University of Montana, Missoula.

http://www.uarizona.edu/~ecubbins/webcrit/html

This website provides guidelines on how to evaluate authenticity of American Indian websites.

http://libits.library.ualberta.ca/library_html/subjects/native_studies/guides/treaties.html

Guide to Canadian treaties with First Nations.

http://www.aics.org/WK/index.html

Documents related to Wounded Knee and Indian resistance, including flyers, newspapers, and other print materials.

http://www2.csusm.edu/nadp/nadp.htm

Documents about Native Americans.

http://anpaserver.uair.edu/RIS/RISWEB.ISA

From the University of Arkansas, this is a bibliography of native writers since 1772.

http://www.nativeshop.org/pro-choice.html

A website on the reproductive rights of indigenous women with a pro-choice focus.

http://www.lib.iun.indiana.edu/trannurs.htm#nativeamer

This contains links to health databases and resources.

http://www.wsu.edu:8080/~amerstu/mw/

Multicultural perspectives on the American West.

http://www.johncom/firstnat/index.html

First Nations tribal information project.

http://members.aol.com/angelawa859/index.html

African-American and Indian genealogy page.

http://www.kennett.co.nz/law/indigenous

Comprehensive site on indigenous peoples and the law.

http://www.cwis.org/wwwvl/indig-vl.html

Library of indigenous resources on the Web.

http://www2.hmc.edu/~tbeckman/indian.html

California Indian resources.

http://usd.edu/iais/indianstudies/bib.html Accesses

University of South Dakota Indian Studies bibliography.

http://sun3.lib.uci/edu/~sica/microform/resources/a/a_063.htm

Information on access to American Indian periodicals on microfiche.

http://www.sims.berkeley.edu/courses/lis190/s96/abaurrea/biblio/htm

A bibliography concerning gambling on reservations through 1994.

http://www.hsc.colorado.edu/sm/nehcrc/library.htm

The American Indian elder health care center resource library on the Web.

http://www.55koy.com/~wildwest/indian.html

American Indian tribal links.

http://ruralinstitute.umt.edu/rtcrural/Indian/Factsheets/US_Govt_Legislation.htm

This is a rural fact sheet on the U.S. Government and American Indians with disabilities. It contains survey information concerning numbers on tribal members with disabilities, accessibility, and resources.

http://ruralinstitute.umt.edu/rtcrural/Indian/Factsheets/AIDL_History.htm

A brief history of U.S. law with respect to American Indians.

http://ruralinstitute.umt.edu/rtcrural/Indian/Factsheets/disability_laws.htm

This is a summary of disability law, with attention to American Indians and government response.

http://www-library.stanford.edu/depts/ssrg/native/appe.html

A list of basic readings on 500 years of contact.

http://www.ncai.org/indianissues/Housing/sencomstat.htm

Statement of President of National Congress of American Indians, Ron Allen, regarding housing programs.

http://www.welfareinfo.org/tribalresource.htm

Resources for Welfare Decisions, Volume 3, Issue 5 (September, 1999). This site provides a wealth of information on tribal TANF and welfare-to-work programs. This website lists studies of the impact of welfare to work programs on various communities, with contact information including telephone numbers and/or web addresses. It includes a section on the activities of various organizations, including the National Congress of American Indians, as well as providing contact information for various resources such as BIA, U.S. Senate Committee on Indian Affairs, and many others. There is a brief introductory description of tribal TANF and welfare to work programs.

http://www-sul.stanford.edu/depts/ssrg/adams/shortcu/films/amindfilms.html

> **American Indian Studies Films at Stanford University.** This is a guide to selected films and videos focusing on Native Americans held by this university. However, the information may be useful to those who wish to compile a listing of films and videos for classroom or other purposes or access visual materials through interlibrary loan. Documentaries, features, short films, and reference works are categorized by type.